Contents

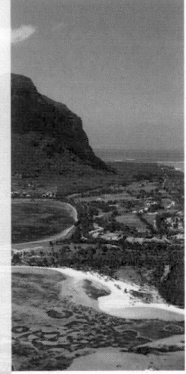

Introduction

'You gather the idea that Mauritius was made first then heaven; heaven being copied after Mauritius.'

MARK TWAIN (1835–1910)

With powder-white Indian Ocean beaches and a turquoise sea with dramatic mountain backdrops, year-round sunshine and fantastic hotels, it's perhaps no surprise that Mauritius is referred to as the 'jewel' of the Indian Ocean.

Dream holidays are this island's forte. Mauritius not only offers the best standard of hotel service in the Indian Ocean, it also has world-class spas and golf courses, top chefs serving mouth-watering multi-ethnic cuisine and, unlike many tropical islands, plenty to see and do.

The tourism board promotes Mauritius with the tagline, 'So many reasons'. The island's key selling point is its beaches, and many visitors can't bear to leave them. It's also a watersports mecca, with everything imaginable from undersea walks to diving and snorkelling on the coral reef, as well as deep-sea fishing, windsurfing and sailing. Yet beyond the beach, the island's wide swathes of natural beauty have a lot to offer those who want to get out and about. Rolling fields of sugar cane bleached by the sun are interspersed with lush green mountains to climb. There's trekking through inland forests that have soaring ebony trees, home to some of the world's

rarest birds. Beautiful flowers, such as hibiscus and bougainvillea and the ubiquitous red anthurium, fill hotel gardens. As if all that weren't enough, in the last 15 years or so Mauritius has

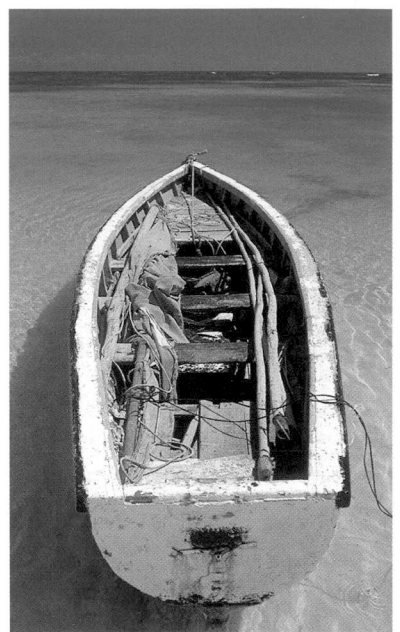

The sparkling turquoise waters of Mauritius

Pieter Both mountain in the Moka Range

developed eco-adventures, which mean getting on a quad bike or in a 4WD, or cycling, horse riding or even ziplining to explore its green interior. What's more, there are no venomous snakes and insects or dangerous animals to spoil a holiday, and English is conveniently spoken by people in the tourism industry to make the living easy.

From its swashbuckling history of piracy and shipwrecks, the island's colonial years brought a fascinating fusion of cultures to Mauritius – French, Indian, Chinese and Creole.

The people here are also special, giving the island a relaxed, lively and friendly vibe. Multiculturalism informs everything from dress to dancing, and buildings to breakfast. Cultural sites range from colonial monuments and architecture to riotous Indian temples, bustling markets and fascinating religious festivals. However, what visitors notice most is a culture infused with a deep hospitality, where nothing is too much trouble, and the kindness and thoughtfulness of local people stay with guests a long time after they return home.

The land

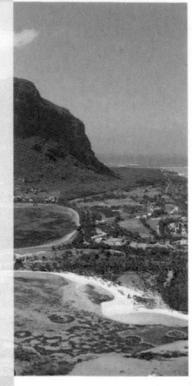

About 8 million years ago, the pear-shaped volcanic island of Mauritius rose out of the Indian Ocean. Around 2,000km (1,240 miles) off the southeastern coast of Africa, Mauritius lies east of Madagascar. Along with Rodrigues and Réunion, it forms part of the Mascarene Islands. These islands, away from major sea trading routes, remained isolated and uninhabited by humans for thousands of years, allowing them to evolve a unique flora and fauna.

Today, Mauritius is recognised as one of the world's biodiversity hotspots, and much of it has been designated as a protected area.

Mauritius is a decent size for a tropical island, at 45km (28 miles) wide and 65km (40 miles) long and covering 1,865sq km (720sq miles). Its 320km (200 miles) of coastline is surrounded by a clear blue lagoon, mostly ringed by the world's third-largest coral reef. And, in the interior, it can be seen how the local 'Green Island' rum got its name.

Explosions and weathering left the island with crater walls at Black River, Grand Port and Moka. Further eruptions, about 4 million years ago, formed the crater at Trou aux Cerfs (overlooking Curepipe) and the crater lake at Grand Bassin. The last major volcanic activity, which was just over 100,000 years ago, created the coastal plains. The island is sheltered by barriers of coral reefs forming crystal-clear lagoons, and uninhabited islets that have been important refuges for wildlife are scattered around the coast.

Mauritius is dominated by a central plateau lying at about 650m (2,133ft) above sea level, all that is left of a vast crater, and surrounded by the mountainous crust of the crater wall – three mountain ranges rising just over 800m (2,625ft) from the sea, forming the island's backbone. These mostly velvety volcanic peaks poke out of the sugar-cane plantations that until recently provided the island's key livelihood. The peaks' steep slopes drop towards a mostly cultivated coastal plain and down to the sea.

In contrast, the northern part of the island is a wide plain, and a flat margin surrounds most of the island. The coast is largely bordered by imported *filao* (casuarina) trees, but bleached plains such as those at Yemen (*see pp48–9*) are a reminder of nearby Africa.

The dodo

Mauritius' relative isolation led to the development of a unique flora and fauna, including the dodo. The dodo is Mauritius' national emblem and part of the island's identity, although the bird was extinct by the end of the 17th century.

The Portuguese named the dodo in 1500. Identified through DNA samples as a large pigeon, the name may have been given because it cooed 'doo doo'. Eyewitness accounts, mainly from sailors passing through, described the large, flightless, waddling birds as similar to swans, but with none of the elegance. Clues suggest the dodo was grey or grey-brown, with a few black quills for wings and coloured plumes sprouting from its tail. Popular myth portrays the dodo as plump, but in

Wall decoration in Dodo Square, Grand Baie

fact it ran very fast, and the myth may have been based on those birds transported to Europe in a confined space and fed on ship's biscuits!

The dodo's flightlessness developed over millions of years of evolution. It had no predators before humans, and, with fruits and berries, leaves and bulbous roots on or near the ground, it didn't need to fly to find food. It had a strong beak and was thought to swallow large stones to help grind food.

In 1638, the Dutch occupied Mauritius, and its once impenetrable ebony forests were destroyed in order to make way for imported crops such as sugar cane, rice, tobacco, indigo, vegetables and citrus trees. Sailors, invalids, convicts and slaves followed, and the defenceless dodo was an easy target for hunters, although, by all accounts, the meat had a nauseating taste.

An even more deadly threat to dodo eggs and chicks were the rats and monkeys that escaped from ships. They could reach the nests, built about 40cm (16in) above the ground with their single egg. Deer, pigs, goats, chickens, dogs and cats were all introduced to the island, each

A dodo and chick

making life more difficult for the dodo. Slowly, the sanctuary that had sheltered this unusual bird for at least a million years of evolution was destroyed. By 1690, less than 100 years after humans arrived, the dodo was extinct.

It wasn't until 1865 that dodo bones were found, by accident, in the marsh of Mare Aux Songes, proving that the dodo was not just a figment of sailors' imaginations. Further bones were found in 2005–6, the first since the 1920s. In 2008, the Natural History Museum in Port Louis created a Dodo Gallery for exhibits.

Two dodo skeletons are also found in the Mauritius Museum Council there, and fine busts can be seen in La Vanille Réserve des Mascareignes and Île aux Aigrettes, possibly its last resting place. At Casela Nature and Leisure Park, visitors can see the Nicobar Pigeon, the dodo's closest living relative. Pockets of original forest lie in the Black River Gorges and at Petrin, where you can see The Tambalacoque or 'dodo tree'. However, you will find the most dodos carved in wood, cast in metal, made into soft toys and depicted on paintings and postcards. Pictures of dodos are sewn on everything from T-shirts to towels, and you can even find dodo cocktails, drunk out of a porcelain dodo figurine.

For the full story of this improbable bird, read *Dodo – the Bird behind the Legend* (IPC Mauritius, ISBN 978-9-99033-815-7) by Alan Grihault, or visit *www.dodosite.com*

History

500 BC Phoenician sailors from the Red Sea come down the east coast of Africa and visit places in the Indian Ocean.

AD 900–1000 Arabs trade along the African coast and probably visit Mauritius. In the Middle Ages, Mauritius appears on maps with an Arabic name, Dina Arobi (Eastern Island).

1488 The Portuguese explorer Bartolomeu Dias is the first recorded European to sail from the Cape of Good Hope into the Indian Ocean.

1500 Mauritius is accidentally discovered by Diogo Dias, Bartolomeu's brother, when his ship is blown off course by a storm.

1507 The island is named by Domingo Fernandez Pereira, after his ship, *Isla do Cerne* (Swans' Island), but also perhaps after the swan-like dodos on the island.

1513 A Portuguese sailor, Pedro Mascarenhas, gives the name 'Mascarenes' to the group of islands that are today known as Mauritius, Réunion and Rodrigues.

1528 Another Portuguese sailor, Diogo Rodrigues, gives his name to Rodrigues. The name has stuck.

1598 A Dutch squadron arrive at Vieux Grand Port, in the southeast of the island, naming it Mauritius in honour of Prince Maurits van Nassau of Holland.

1638–1710 The Dutch settle on Mauritius, but only for 20 years. Another attempt at settlement is made, but they finally leave the island in 1710, and also their legacy: sugar cane, deer and monkeys. The dodo is destroyed and the ebony forest plundered.

1715 The French arrive and call the island 'Île de France'. Governor Mahé de La Bourdonnais establishes Port Louis as a naval base and builds a road network. Slaves are imported from Africa and Madagascar.

1744	The ship *Le Saint-Géran* sinks during a violent storm, and inspires the 18th-century novel *Paul et Virginie* by Bernardin de Saint-Pierre.
1797	In the census, the population of Mauritius is 59,020, of which 6,237 are whites, 3,703 are free men and 49,080 are slaves.
1810	The British colonise the island during the Napoleonic Wars but agree, unusually, to respect French language, laws and culture, and to allow the French to keep their lands, which they still own today.
1810–1968	British influence leads to economic and social change. Abolishing slavery in 1835, indentured labourers are brought from India to work in the sugar-cane fields, which becomes the main industry. Chinese and Muslim traders arrive. Communications are improved.
1835–1936	Indian labourers had few rights, but conditions are improved by the setting up of a royal commission to look into immigration, and a visit by Mahatma Gandhi in 1907.
1936–68	Sir Seewoosagur Ramgoolam, founder of the Labour Party, leads the fight for independence, which Mauritius gains in 1968.
1968–86	Sir Seewoosagur Ramgoolam is prime minister until his death in 1986, and many buildings are named in his honour.
1970s–90s	Successful diversification from sugar to textiles and tourism has a big impact on the economy.
1992	Mauritius becomes a republic, although it still forms part of the British Commonwealth.
2008	Mauritius celebrates 40 years of independence. Le Morne Brabant is declared a UNESCO World Heritage Site.
2010	Mauritius becomes a duty-free shopping haven. Bicentenary of the Battle of Grand Port.

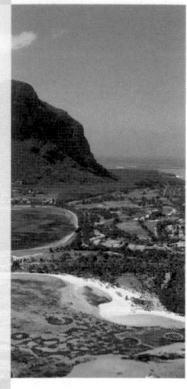

Politics

Mauritius achieved independence from the UK in 1968, becoming a republic within the British Commonwealth in 1992. A democratic state based on the British pattern of government, it has 62 members of parliament elected every five years. A president presides over government, headed by the prime minister. The island enjoys political stability, although it suffers from corruption and is unusual in its preference for government by coalition, perhaps reflecting the national multicultural ethos.

The Mauritius Labour Party (MLP) headed by Sir Seewoosagur Ramgoolam (*see box below*) took over at Independence, and faced problems of overpopulation, unemployment and a mono-crop economy. Sir Seewoosagur established the export-processing zone that became crucial to Mauritius' future growth through foreign investment.

Independence also saw the return of Paul Bérenger, an extreme left-wing Franco-Mauritian whose aim was the redistribution of wealth on the island. His party, the Mouvement Militant Mauricien (MMM), rose to power in 1982, headed by Anerood Jugnauth, a Hindu lawyer. Mauritian politics have seen the same figures and families dominate, in different arrangements as multi-party coalitions, ever since.

Diversification and cooperating with the private sector rescued the economy. This was continued by the Labour government of Dr Navinchandra Ramgoolam, Seewoosagur's son, elected to power in 1995. Paul Bérenger formed an alliance with the MSM (Militant Socialist Movement) and became prime minister in 2003 as the first white, non-Hindu prime minister since Independence. Defeated in 2005, the country is now in the hands of a new party, The Socialist Alliance, headed by Dr Navin Chandra Ramgoolam. May 2010 saw him re-elected for a third term in office.

SIR SEEWOOSAGUR RAMGOOLAM

The most famous and loved of Mauritian politicians, Sir Seewoosagur Ramgoolam is referred to as the 'Father of the Nation'. Born in Mauritius to poor Hindu parents, Seewoosagur trained in medicine in London. Returning to Mauritius in 1955, after 14 years in the UK, he got involved in politics to represent the struggles of the lower classes. Becoming a member of the legislative council, he was elected mayor of Port Louis, and at Independence he became Mauritius' first prime minister. Pamplemousses Gardens and the airport are named after him, and you'll see his picture in even the smallest shack of a restaurant.

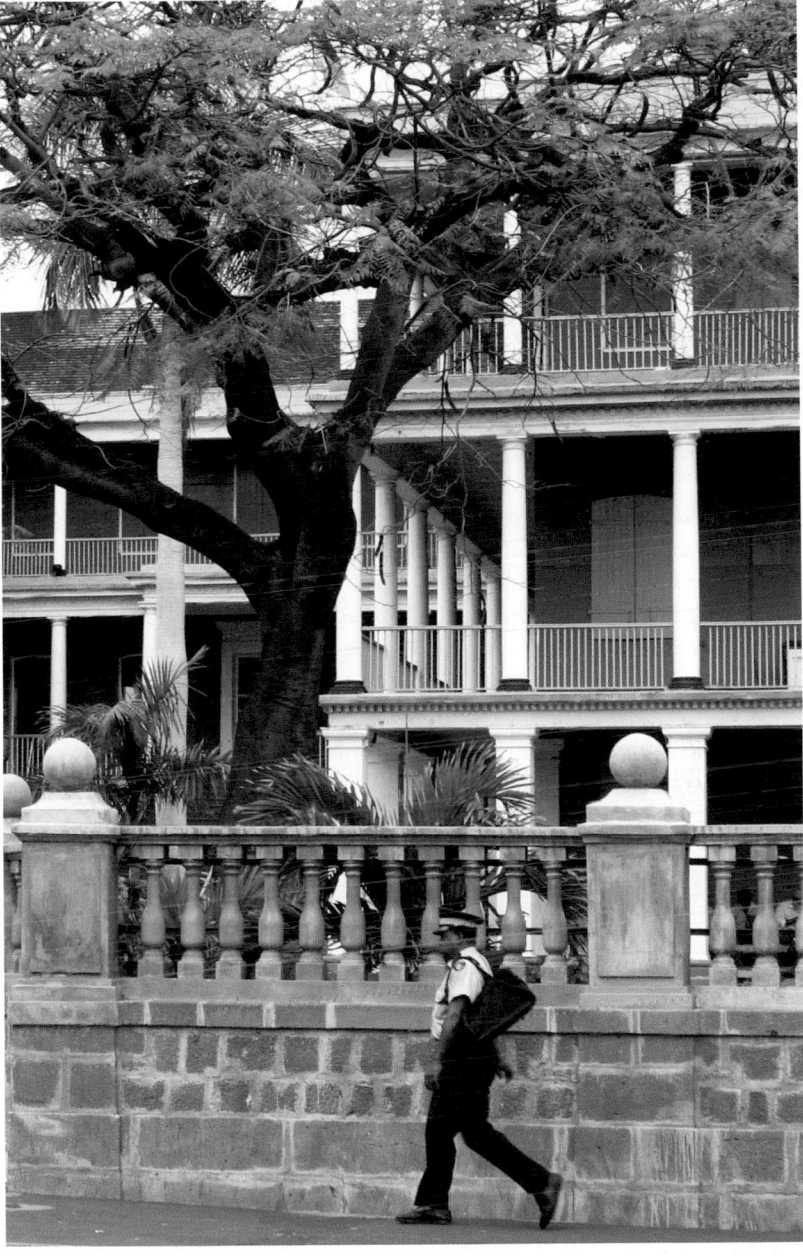

Government House in Port Louis

Culture

Mauritius is one of the most densely populated countries on earth, with around 625 people per sq km (0.39sq miles). It calls itself 'a world in one island', and this vibrant multi-ethnic society of around 1.2 million people is a melting pot of cultures, religions and languages. Mauritians are all immigrants, descended from Indian, African, European and Chinese settlers.

Mauritians of Indian heritage make up almost 70 per cent of the population, some being Tamils and Telugus. They are mostly descended from indentured labourers brought in to work on the sugar cane. Of these, around 50 per cent are Hindu. Indian Muslims, who make up around 16 per cent of the population, came separately as traders.

Europeans are mainly the descendants of French settlers, mostly sugar plantation owners, and are referred to as Franco-Mauritians. The descendants of African and Malagasy slaves, usually mixed with European blood, are referred to as Creoles. Chinese entrepreneurs came after World War II, fleeing the Japanese and then the Communists, and account for over 30,000 of the population. Around 30 per cent of the population – most Franco-Mauritians, Creoles and Chinese – are Christian, the majority Roman Catholic. About 2 per cent of the Chinese population practise traditional Chinese religions, Buddhism and Confucianism.

As 'one people, one nation', according to the national anthem, this coexistence of peoples expresses itself throughout the island. French colonial mansions lie near Indian temples, and the National Store sits next to Chung Choy Snack. It is also seen in Mauritians themselves. Women are as comfortable in saris as Levis, and people as happy eating crêpes and croissants as curries and chapattis.

Ganesh Chaturthi celebrations in Grand Bassin

Fishermen at sunset

In addition, vibrant religious festivals are celebrated throughout the year (*see pp16–17*).

The history of an area partly dictates the ethnicity of a population. Some villages, such as Rivière Noire, have a large Creole population, mostly fishermen, as many left the sugar fields after the abolition of slavery. Floréal and Curepipe both have large Franco-Mauritian communities, and Triolet, with the oldest Hindu temple, a large Indian population. Traditional life is still evident around the island. Women in long boots and straw hats can be seen working in the sugar fields, and a few fishermen still ply the coast in their wooden pirogues.

The arts

As an island far from anywhere, it is perhaps unsurprising that Mauritius offers little for the culture vulture. It has limited cinema and theatre, but music and dance are central to this culture's artistic expression, and the earthy African-slave-inspired Sega (*see pp16–17*) is the most interesting offering. Second is the colonial architecture, evident throughout the island (*see pp50–51*).

Most of the arts follow in the French tradition. The most famous Mauritian literary contribution, a tragi-romantic bestseller in 1778, is *Paul et Virginie* by Frenchman Bernardin de Saint-Pierre. The novel was inspired by the sinking of the ship, *Le Saint-Géran*, in 1744. Paul tries to save his beloved from drowning, but out of modesty she refuses to take off her heavy clothes. She drowns and Paul dies of a broken heart.

Mauritius' best-known sculptor is Prosper d'Epinay, and his classic statue of the star-crossed lovers from the book *Paul et Virginie* can be seen in The Blue Penny Museum in Port Louis (*see p26*). Contemporary Mauritian artists include Vaco Baissac, whose colourful works can be found in his Grand Baie gallery near that of François Vrot, who paints women working in the fields, and there is a host of others.

The Sega

As far back as 1768, travellers were bringing back tales of the Sega (pronounced 'saygah'), the sensual song and dance unique to this island. It came from the African slaves, who traditionally gathered by firelight on the beach dancing to a rhythmic drumbeat at the end of a hard working day. Now mixed with other influences, the hip movements a little Latin and the hand movements Southeast Asian, it is the national dance of Mauritius. Every Mauritian knows the vibrant Sega, and it is

The Sega danced at La Pirogue resort

traditionally danced at family gatherings, festivals and celebrations.

This is a dance of the hips, which sway and gyrate to the pounding rhythm of the *ravane*, a goat's hide drum tightened over a flame and described as sounding like 'a husky bark'. Other instruments that make up the unique musical sound are the *maravanne* (a box – this used to be a gourd or *calebasse* – filled with small stones and shaken like maracas) and the metal triangle, tapped with an iron rod to give a high-pitched tingling note (originally the *panga*, used to cut sugar cane). The traditional guitar, a single gut string attached to half a dried pumpkin, has been replaced by the more sophisticated electric guitar. Hypnotic and colourful Creole lyrics about the trials of love or the humour of life rise above the rhythm.

A partnered dance, the man stands with his hands on his hips, while the woman shuffle-steps around him, waving a colourful handkerchief, and with arms outstretched. The couple then face each other, holding at the waist and shoulder. To the cry of *'En Bas! En Bas!'* (Down, Down), both bend their knees and lean backwards

Locals play and dance Sega on the beach

while continuing to gyrate the hips, ending up on the floor. Perhaps because it was once danced in the sand – although some say it is because the slaves were in shackles the feet shuffle and never leave the ground. As the tempo increases, the dance becomes more high-spirited and unrestrained and the dancers jerk, stretch and sway with animated movements to keep pace.

The Sega can be heard around the island, blasting from cars or shops, or where Mauritians gather on public beaches. Ti Frère was the island's most famous traditional Sega star, bringing it back into fashion in the 1950s. Traditional Sega, including Ti Frère's

most popular track, 'Anita', can be seen and heard on YouTube (www. youtube.com). Many young Mauritians now prefer 'seggae' – a new musical form mixing Sega and reggae invented by Creole singer, Kaya, who died under suspicious circumstances in jail and became a national hero.

If you're very lucky, you may see locals dancing the Sega, but otherwise almost all of the big hotels have Sega performances. In colourful costume, the women with cropped tops and billowing skirts, and the men in loud shirts and pedal pushers, these shows accentuate the eroticism of the dance. Be warned – guests are usually asked to join in!

Festivals and events

With a multi-ethnic population, Mauritius has year-round religious festivals, from the colour and riotousness of Holi to the seriously devout Cavadi. The following is a list of the major festivals that take place on the island. For a complete listing, visit www.mauritius.net

January/February

Cavadi This is perhaps the most devout and dramatic of the Mauritian festivals, celebrated by Indians of Tamil origin. It is about purifying devotees from evil, and devotees walk to the temple in a trance with their tongue, chest and cheeks pierced with needles and tiny mugs of purification milk hanging from hooks off their backs. On their shoulders, for penitence, is the Cavadi, an arc decorated with flowers symbolising the sacred mountains.

Chinese New Year/Spring Festival The most important festival for the Chinese-Mauritian community. They clean their homes, exchange traditional wax cakes and light firecrackers to chase away evil spirits. Chinese dragons and lion dances parade through Port Louis' Chinatown, and red, a symbol of happiness, is everywhere.

February

Maha Shivaratree 'The great night of Shiva' is the largest Hindu festival outside India. This is when the island's Hindu devotees, dressed in white, make a pilgrimage to Grand Bassin where they leave offerings of food and flowers in Shiva's honour.

March

Holi Possibly the most spectacular festival is the Hindu festival of joy, held at Grand Bassin. People splash each

MULTI-FAITH MAURITIUS – HINDU GODS

Small shrines can be found in the sugar-cane forests and by the sea around the island. Hindu or Telugu temples are predominantly red, whereas the Tamil ones are yellow. The main Hindu gods are Ganesh, the elephant god who stands for intelligence and wisdom, Shiva the creator, and the goddess Durga (known as Kali to Tamils) who protects against evil, and are worshipped in the temples from mid-September to October. There's also Hanuman, the monkey god, who represents power and strength, and Lakshmi, goddess of Light, worshipped at Diwali (October/November). Tamils' main creator is Lord Muruga, worshipped at Cavadi.

PRAYER DAYS

Hindus have special prayer and vegetarian fasting days on Tuesday, Thursday and Friday; these are the liveliest days to visit the temples.

other with coloured water, throw lurid coloured powder and wish each other luck.

Ougadi This is a celebration of New Year by the Telugu Hindus.

May/June
Corpus Christi Devout Roman Catholics parade through the streets of Port Louis.

August/September
Ganesh Chaturthi This is a Hindu celebration of the birthday of Ganesh, god of Wisdom. In Baie du Cap, processions take statues of Ganesh to the sea, and others take their statues for a dunking at Grand Bassin.

September
Father Laval Day People of all faiths make a pilgrimage to the tomb of Father Laval at Sainte Croix, Port Louis, on 9 September, the anniversary of his death. A French priest who lived in the 19th century and protected slaves here, he is a symbol of compassion and is said to have healing powers.

October/November
Diwali An Indian festival, Diwali celebrates the victory of Lord Rama over the devil (as depicted in the epic

poem, the *Ramayana*) and uplifting of spiritual darkness. Also known as the festival of light, it's a pretty sight – with small oil lamps shining everywhere to guide the goddess of wealth and good fortune to homes.

November
Ganga Asnan This is the time the Hindu community bathes in the sea for purification, as they would have done in the Ganges in India. It can be seen at main beaches around the island.

November/December
Id al-Fitr This marks the end of Ramadan for the island's Muslims, and is celebrated with prayers at the mosque and with feasting.

December to February
Teemeedee After ten days of purification and praying, Tamil penitents walk across a pit of burning coals in certain temples across the island, before cooling their feet in milk.

Religious icons for sale in Port Louis

Highlights

Page	
26	The north
46	The west
76	The east

Île aux Serpents

Île Ronde

Île Plate

Îlot Gabriel

Rodrigues ❸ Island

Indian Ocean

Coin de Mire

Cap Malheureux

Pointe aux Canonniers

Grand Baie ❾

Trou aux Biches

Île d'Ambre

Triolet

Pointe aux Piments

Pamplemousses

Belle Mare Plage

❿ PORT LOUIS

Le Pouce ▲ 812

Pieter Both ▲ 820

Bon Accueil

Centre de Flacq ❺

Union Flacq

Quartier Militaire

Rivière Sèche Bel Air

Île aux Cerfs ❶

Flic en Flac

Quatre Bornes

Phoenix

Montagne Blanche

L'Etoile

Kawal Nagar

Floréal

Curepipe

Tamarin Bay

Tamarin

Henrietta

Midlands

Eau Bleue Reservoir

Anse Jonchée

Grande Rivière Noire

Banane ❼

Vieux Grand Port

Petite Rivière Noire

❻

Black River Gorges National Park

Grand Bassin ❹

Grand Bois

Mahébourg

Île aux Aigrettes

Chamarel

Le Morne Brabant ▲ 555

Bassin Blanc

Piton Savanne ▲ 704

Sir Seewoosagur Ramgoolam ❽ ✈

Blue Bay

❷

Baie du Cap

Bel Ombre

St Aubin

Rivière des Anguilles

Souillac

Gris Gris

N

① **Lazing around on Île aux Cerfs**, an idyllic island surrounded by a sand bar on the glamorous east coast (*see pp79 & 82*).

② **Driving along the wild south coast**, where waves crash dramatically against basalt cliffs, and sleepy fishing villages lie along pristine bays (*see pp72–3 & 88–9*).

③ **A trip to Rodrigues Island**, where the chillis are hot but the people and pace of life chilled (*see p105*).

④ **Attending a festival at Grand Bassin**, equivalent to the holy Ganges for Mauritian Hindus (*see pp68–9*).

⑤ **A luxury spa treatment** at one of the island's fabulous hotels. With a number of top names, including The Residence, to choose from, Mauritius has become a spa-lover's paradise (*see pp136–7*).

⑥ **A trip to Black River Gorges National Park**, the forested centre of the island, and the place to see indigenous plants and wildlife (*see pp58–63*).

⑦ **Domaine des 7 Vallées**, an eco-estate, for a quad bike ride to a waterfall and an adventurous lunch of wild boar or deer curry with a stupendous view (*see p79*).

⑧ **A helicopter ride** over the island will give you a fantastic view of the volcanic mountains, the patterns of sugar fields and the reef from above (*see p108*).

⑨ **Grand Baie**, for nightlife, entertainment and shops as well as some of the best beaches and watersports on the island (*see p36*).

⑩ **Port Louis' Central Market** and the **Caudan Waterfront** to bag a few bargains to take home (*see pp27–9*).

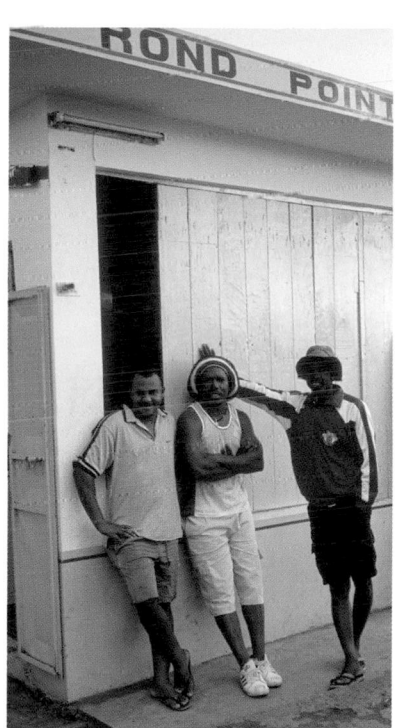

Locals chilling on Rodrigues Island

Suggested itineraries

As Mauritius is a small island, it may come as a surprise to some visitors that getting around takes time. With only one major highway from north to south, most driving is along narrow roads, often through congested towns, with dogs and people spilling out on to the streets. Even travelling from the airport at the southeasterly tip to Cap Malheureux along the highway takes 90 minutes, so bear this in mind when you set off exploring.

Exploring

As Mauritius is a long way from anywhere, most international visitors come for a week or two, ample time to sample what the island has to offer beyond the beach. The key to exploring is to visit places in the same region, doing a chunk at a time. A day or half day is easily spent, sometimes at one attraction. Excursions from the hotel by minibus are the easiest and most convenient way to tour the island, and the most popular option (*see pp102–3*) takes you to both land and sea attractions. Otherwise, options are to take a taxi or hire a car for the day, which allows for more stop-offs and adventures.

Itineraries

There are interesting attractions in every region of the island, so how to choose? Most visitors head to hotspots in the north, such as the capital, Port Louis, Grand Baie and surrounds; the west for family-friendly beaches, Casela Nature and Leisure Park, Yemen Nature Escapade and specialist activities such as diving and deep-sea fishing; and the east regions for glamour, beaches and the offshore island of Île aux Cerfs. Although with few beaches for swimming, there are major attractions in the southeast and southwest. This constitutes off the beaten track, giving an insight into natural, traditional and historic areas of Mauritius.

If visiting for a week, and wanting a general feel for Mauritius, a key place to include on an itinerary is the island

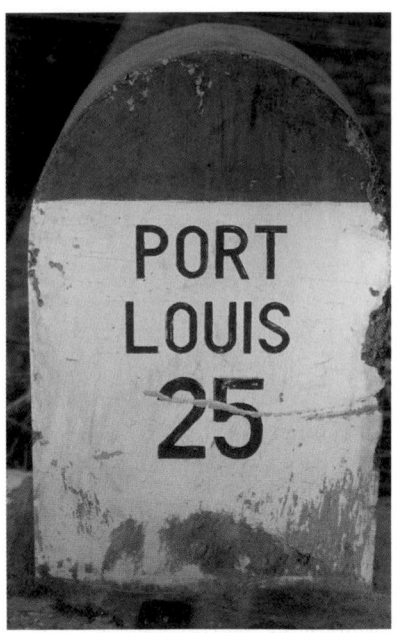

An old mile post to the capital, Port Louis

A flamboyant tree overhangs a road in the north of the island

playground of Île aux Cerfs in the east – the most accessible and most popular excursion provides swimming on a sand bar, rum punch, and a whole range of watersports or a game of golf in one of the world's most stunning settings. As a day or half-day excursion, it can be combined with other beautiful beaches on this coast such as Belle Mare, and perhaps a spa treatment, or at least a cocktail, in one of the island's most glamorous hotels.

In the north, the capital, Port Louis, and Grand Baie top everyone's hit list. Port Louis has the sophisticated and most traditional shopping as well as main museums and key cultural and historical sites. As suggested on page 32, it's best seen on a walking tour, which

takes a morning. It's easy to spend a whole day here, but most people head to Pamplemousses Botanical Gardens, which is on every excursion's itinerary. If visiting independently, it's a good idea to lunch at either L'Aventure du Sucre or Domaine Les Pailles, having seen the surrounding attractions first, and visit Pamplemousses later in the afternoon. Otherwise, climb up Le Pouce in a couple of hours for great views over the capital.

Grand Baie has shops too, but more interesting here are its many kilometres of great beaches all within a short drive of each other, and a whole range of excursions both above and below the water. It's a mix of moods, from the tranquil northerly point of Cap

The church of Notre Dame Auxiliatrice, Cap Malheureux

Malheureux, which, along with taking a catamaran to the Northern Islands, is a place to get away from it all, to the bustling hub of Grand Baie with its nightlife, restaurants and entertainment. Places of historical significance are a little lost here between the sophisticated hotels on quiet peninsulas and the beach bungalows and budget hotels. For those wanting to get away, you can kayak around Île d'Ambre where *Le Saint-Géran* sank or mountain bike in a nature reserve.

A catamaran cruise to see the dolphins in Tamarin Bay in the west is popular with families and couples. Also in the west is Casela Nature and Leisure Park, another family favourite, and, next to it, Yemen, an African-style savanna and the place to try quad biking or trekking at the base of one of Mauritius' mountains. Being the 'sunset coast', this is also the coast for a sunset cruise.

In the southwest, the main highlight is the Black River Gorges National Park up on the uninhabited plateau of Plaine Champagne. Most people stop at a couple of lookouts and Grand Bassin, the holy lake for the Hindus that is best seen with a guide. However, nature-lovers could spend a day or half day walking here in Mauritius' largest forest. If your time is limited, combine a trip here, as many excursions do, with shopping in the inland towns such as Curepipe and Floréal en route.

If more in the mood for eco-adventure, a visit to Domaine des 7 Vallées is recommended, or dip down to Chamarel Coloured Earth. Hitting the southwest coast, one of the prettiest routes on the island passes Baie du Cap and Souillac to reach Gris Gris, a wild but accessible spot where waves bash against the black volcanic rocks. If you prefer eco-adventure to the more commercial attraction of Chamarel, head to the newest nature reserve on this coast, Valriche Nature Reserve at Bel Ombre, for quad biking, 4WD excursions and trekking, or just a great lunch at the château.

The southeast is Mauritius at its most characterful. Culture and history abound in Mahébourg and Vieux Grand Port. A lunch stop-off with panoramic views is Domaine d'Anse Jonchée and the Ylang Ylang farm, which won't take long, and while near this coast a highlight has to be snorkelling or taking a glass-bottom boat excursion over Blue Bay Marine Park. If there is time and you are a nature-lover (*see opposite*), visit the nature reserve of Île aux Aigrettes, a five-minute boat ride from this coast. If you've got a family, the mini-zoo of La Vanille Réserve des Mascareignes further west is a must.

Time permitting, a trip to one of the offshore islands – the Northern Islands are the most popular – will give you a feeling of getting away from it all. If you have three weeks or you are on a second visit, a trip to Rodrigues, 'the anti-stress island' and a Mauritius of 50 years ago, is a relaxing treat.

The high street in sleepy Port Mathurin, Rodrigues Island

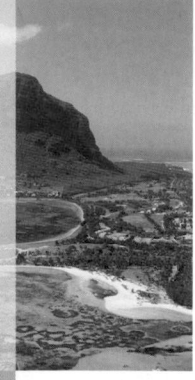

The north

The north has more sunny days than anywhere else in Mauritius, and many of the island's best beaches. It's perhaps then no surprise that it is the tourism hub of the island, centred on the beach town of Grand Baie which has hot shopping, a dense concentration of hotels and the most après-sol entertainment. In contrast, the secluded Northern Islands offer a chance to get away from it all. Then there's the centre of culture, and shopping, Mauritius' bustling port capital, Port Louis.

PORT LOUIS

Pronounced either 'Port Lewis' or 'Por Loowee', Mauritius' port capital on the northwest coast is cradled by an amphitheatre of mountains. It was in this sheltered spot with a superior harbour that Mahé de La Bourdonnais (*see p10*) founded the capital of Île de France, superseding Mahébourg. The city is laid out in rectangular

A VALUABLE MISTAKE

In September 1847, the wife of the Lieutenant-Governor of Mauritius, Sir William Gomm, was seeking an original way to invite guests to their Annual Ball. Summoning a local jeweller and watchmaker, she asked him to produce 500 one-penny and 500 two-penny stamps. Having carefully engraved the stamps on to a copper plate, the jeweller copied the design from the English stamps bearing Queen Victoria's head, then engraved 'Mauritius' on the right and 'Post Office' on the left. No one noticed that 'Post Office' had been written instead of 'Post Paid' until after the invitations had been posted. The mistake made the Blue Penny stamp one of the most valuable in the world.

blocks, making it easy to get around on foot. Street sellers peddling everything from *dholl purri* and croissants to Chinese slippers stand on cracked pavements in front of the graceful colonial buildings which vie with modern skyscrapers and sophisticated shopping in the Port Louis of today. Mauritius' religious diversity is most evident here in churches and cathedrals, Chinese and Indian temples and a mosque.

Caudan Waterfront

Built in 1996 on a piece of land jutting out into the harbour which was once home to some disused warehouses, this is now the place to find the city's most sophisticated shops and dine within sight of the harbour (*see pp151–2*).
Port Louis Harbour. Tel: 211 6560. www.caudan.com. Open: Mon–Sat 9.30am–5.30pm, Sun 9.30am–noon. Go by excursion, hire car or taxi. Good parking and disabled access.

Blue Penny Museum

The first colonial stamp in the world was issued by Mauritius on 21 September 1847, the Blue Penny stamp. Now one of the most valuable stamps in the world, it can be seen here. Mauritius was the fifth country in the world to use 'sticky' postage stamps. Visitors can follow a postal and historical journey through Mauritian heritage at this excellent interactive museum, its centrepiece an envelope with two rare stamps together, bought for US$3.3 million. There's also a good exhibition of art and whimsy relating to Paul and Virginie (*see p15*), and information on the history of Port Louis.

Caudan Waterfront. Tel: 210 8176.
Open: Mon–Sat 10am–5pm.
Closed: Sun. Audio guides available.
Admission charge.

Central Market

Built in 1884, Port Louis' vibrant Central Market is a meeting place for

BOOK AHEAD

If you're thinking of combining shopping and sightseeing with some eco-adventure, think ahead. Many of the eco-estates or 'Domaines' that offer this need up to 48 hours' notice.

Mauritians looking for tea, curry, fruit, vegetables, herbs and local gossip, and it is the one most visited by tourists. The lovely Victorian wrought-iron gates at the entrance lead into an Eastern atmosphere and experience. There is the widest variety of local and imported arts and crafts, such as *pareos* (sarongs), coloured baskets, linen and silk clothing and cushions, bedspreads and clothes from India, leatherwork and spices.

The food hall is one of the best, and certainly most atmospheric, places to try local Mauritian specialities such as *dholl purri* (pancakes filled with ground peas and served with curry), *gâteaux piments* (chilli cakes) or a biriani, and it is now the only place in the city to find the traditional *alooda* (a flavoured iced milk with black seeds that swell up like sago). The indoor section was renovated in 2004 and souvenir stalls added upstairs, but the market has retained its character with uneven pavements, crowds bargaining hard and fragrant aromas. Start in the new market and then walk to the stalls outside, exiting on Bourbon Street.

Items for sale in the craft market at Caudan Waterfront

Between rue de la Reine and Farquhar Street. Open: Mon–Sat 6am–6pm, Sun 6am–noon.

Champ de Mars racecourse

Founded in 1812, what started as a French military parade ground is now the second-oldest race club in the world. Nestled below the Moka Mountains, it used to be a favourite place to promenade. Now, joining a race day is an opportunity to mix with the locals. *Mauritius Turf Club, Eugène Laurent Street. Tel. 208 6047/729 9621. www.mauritiusturfclub.com. Races: May–Nov Sat & some Sun. Admission charge.*

Chinatown

Mauritius' Chinatown may have lost a lot of the richness of its past, but it's worth a meander along its slightly dilapidated streets to experience its flavour. It's perhaps only in multi-faith Mauritius that the Jummah Mosque, the most important on the island, could be found at Chinatown's edge. Try **Swatow Store** (*54 Royal Street. Tel: 242 0968. Open: daily 9am–4.30pm*) for authentic Chinese crafts, and the area's most famous restaurant, **Lai Min** (*58 Royal Street. Tel. 242 0042. Open: daily 11.30am–2.30pm & 6.30–9.30pm*), for a reasonably priced meal. *Walking north up Royal Street will take you through Chinatown, which stretches across seven blocks from Jummah Mosque Street to Étienne Pellereau Street.*

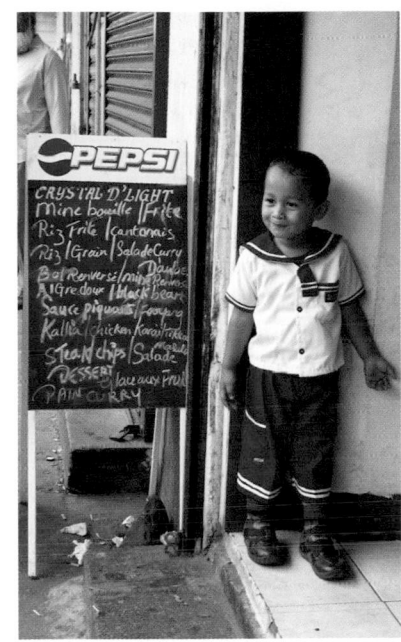

A mix of cultures in Chinatown

Citadel/Fort Adelaide

This sturdy basalt fort, perched on an 86m (282ft) hill overlooking Port Louis, was started by the French and completed by the British in 1834. Unusually, it wasn't built because an outside attack was feared, but because of the enemy within – a French rebellion against the abolition of slavery. However, it was never used. The fort is empty inside, apart from housing

HOLY ETIQUETTE

Tourists should show due respect when visiting religious places. Wear appropriate clothing, not shorts or swimsuits, and remove leather shoes and belts when entering a place of worship.

The Natural History Museum is housed in the Mauritius Institute

the history of the fort, and, upstairs, an incongruous dodo art gallery. The upstairs walkway gives a good overview of Port Louis.

At the end of Jummah Mosque Street heading away from the harbour, too far to walk, but a short taxi ride from the centre.

EXCURSION

Climbing Signal Mountain

This hill at the city's western edge takes its name from the antennae perched on top of it. The road to the summit is blocked off to traffic, but it's an hour's easy walk. At 323m (1,060ft) high, this is a great spot to get a 360-degree view of Port Louis. The best time to go is at about 4pm – return as the sun is setting and watch the lights come on over Port Louis.

Start from the car park opposite Labourdonnais Street, near Marie Reine de Paix.

Government House

Started by Mahé de Labourdonnais in 1738, this elegant colonial building was completed by the British in 1810 and is fronted by a statue of Queen Victoria. Not open to the public, as it's still the centre of government, it is best admired from the top of Place d'Armes, which is opposite.

Opposite Place d'Armes, at the meeting of Royal and Chaussée streets. Closed to the public.

Mauritius Photographic Museum

This museum has hundreds of fascinating photographs showing the history of the island, a collection of old tribal masks from three continents, and photographic and other memorabilia, including the island's first printing press. The photographer-collector who runs it is as interesting as his exhibits.
5 rue du Vieux Conseil. Tel: 211 1705. http://voyaz.com/musee-photo. Open: Mon–Fri 9am–3pm. Closed: Sat & Sun. Admission charge.

Natural History Museum

This is the oldest public museum in Mauritius. Opened in 1842, the Natural History Museum's most famous exhibits are its dodo skeletons, the only ones in Mauritius, housed in a new Dodo Gallery on the first floor. It's a good place to see endemic and introduced animals, and marine life, to learn about cyclones, and to see local woods, fruits and flowers as well as coral, tortoises and insects.

Pick up a cheap, quick snack from the stalls outside and sit in the shade of the banyan trees in the pretty Jardin de la Compagnie (Company Gardens) opposite the museum.
Mauritius Institute, La Chaussée. Tel: 212 0639. http://mauritiusmuseums.com. Open: Mon, Tue, Thur & Fri 9am–4pm, Sat 9am–noon. Closed: Wed & Sun. Guided tours available. Free admission.

Pieter Both Mountain

This mountain, part of the Moka range sheltering Port Louis, is named

MULTI-FAITH MAURITIUS

Port Louis is the best place to see Mauritius' religious diversity, and guided tours focus on this aspect. The white and green Jummah Mosque has priceless carved teak doors inlaid with ivory and an elegant spired dome. The red and gold Confucian Lam Soon Temple was built in the 19th century, and near the racecourse stands the Shree Vishnu Kchetra Temple in a peaceful spot. The white wedding-cake-style Marie Reine de la Paix can also be found nearby, a sacred Catholic monument visited by Pope John Paul II. From the Citadel, there's a view over the Gothic-style Catholic St Louis Cathedral and the wooden Anglican St James Cathedral nearby, which was built in 1828 with 3m (10ft) thick walls to enable them to withstand cyclones.

after a Dutch ship captain who was shipwrecked in a cyclone in Baie du Tombeau (Tomb Bay) in 1615. Local legend has it that a young goatherd was turned into the huge boulder balanced on the top of the mountain as a punishment for disturbing the fairies.

CAP MALHEUREUX

Lying at the most northerly tip of Mauritius is the peaceful fishing village of Cap Malheureux, or Cape of Misfortune, so-called because of the shipwrecks in this spot. It was here that the British naval force took control of Mauritius in 1810, although it's most visited for the pretty red-roofed Roman Catholic church of Notre Dame Auxiliatrice. There is a charming view
(*Cont. on p36*)

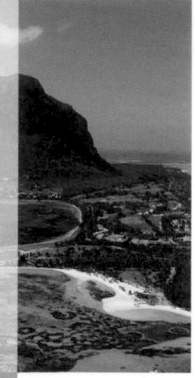

Walk: Port Louis

This walk takes in the main sights of the capital, from its colonial buildings and bustling shopping centres to its religious sites and its most interesting museums. The city is easy to navigate, and everything is within easy walking distance. For the clearest views, less sticky weather and fewer people, the walk is best in the morning.

The walk covers a distance of approximately 2km (1¼ miles) and will take a leisurely 3 hours.

Park at the Caudan Waterfront and begin the walk at the Blue Penny Museum near the entrance.

1 Blue Penny Museum
See pp26–7.
Head into the Caudan Waterfront Centre.

2 Caudan Waterfront Centre
Some of the best shopping on the island, with branches of all the main upmarket shops, duty-free outlets and a craft market.
Turn left at the pirate boat casino and walk along the quay to take the pedestrian underpass to the right just behind Le Petit Gourmet café on to Sir William Newton Street. Take the first left down Farquhar Street.
The entrance to the Central Market is on the right.

3 Central Market
A colourful place to get a taste of local life, have a traditional snack and buy souvenirs.

Start in the new market and then walk through the old one, coming out on Bourbon Street and heading straight up it to turn left on Royal Street to Chinatown.

4 Chinatown and Jummah Mosque
The pretty white and pale green Jummah Mosque marks the edge of Chinatown, which still has some Chinese shops, restaurants and street names.
Retrace your steps and walk down Royal Street until you reach a busy three-lane road. The Government House on the left, opposite the statues of Place d'Armes, is best seen from this side of the road.

5 Government House
See p30.
Continue on down Chaussée Street, one of the oldest, to the Mauritius Institute with its entrance in Poudrière Street.

6 Mauritius Institute
Pop into the capital's Natural History Museum to see the Dodo Gallery there.

Walk through the stringy Banyan trees of the Jardin de la Compagnie, before turning left on to Brown Sequard Street and right on to Poudrière Street. Turn left into Vieux Conseil Street, which is lined with stunning old wooden colonial buildings. In one of them, on your left at the bend, is the Mauritius Photographic Museum.

7 Mauritius Photographic Museum

See p31.

Pass Le Vieux Conseil Restaurant, a popular lunch spot for tourists, on the

left before coming out opposite the Grand Theatre.

8 Grand Theatre

With a colonnaded front, the theatre is as grand as its claim to be the oldest in the southern hemisphere.

With the theatre behind you, return by walking straight down Intendance Street, which becomes Queen Elizabeth Avenue. Turn left on President Kennedy Street and right on Dr A Ferrière Street to take the other pedestrian underpass back to the Caudan Waterfront.

Best beaches

With a turquoise lagoon encircled by a coral reef and 320km (200 miles) of coastline, it's not hard to find a good beach on Mauritius. They really are as idyllic as the brochures promise, with pretty powder-white sand bordering a gentle azure sea. The beaches range from long sweeping stretches of sand to little coves often shaded by casuarina trees or, at hotels bordering the beach, thatched sunshades, making the perfect picture. Although plenty of activities are available to tempt visitors away from the beach, the beaches are still the island's key draw. Beaches are best known for different atmospheres, sports and activities, and it is worth considering this when choosing a hotel.

Theoretically, all beaches are public in Mauritius. In practice, purely public beaches are few, but they are not crowded on weekdays. On a summer weekend evening, you may see Sega played among the snack stalls under the casuarina trees.

Northwest

The largest collection of good public beaches is in the northwest, and will suit those who like a bit of life beside the beach. There is also the largest selection of varied water-based activities and excursions. **Grand Baie** is a beach for hanging out or getting active. It offers an array of watersports including windsurfing, waterskiing and sailing, and, uniquely, parasailing, as well as deep-sea fishing. There are lively après-beach shops, trendy bars, restaurants and clubs. The very popular but small cove of **Péreybère**, off the road between Grand Baie and Cap Malheureux, is backed by a few palm trees and *gajak* (snack) sellers and best visited on weekdays. Many people now head to **Mont Choisy**, a 2km (1¼-mile) narrow white stretch of sand curving north along a turquoise bay from Trou aux Biches to Grand Baie. **Trou aux Biches** means 'Hole of the Does', and it's where female deer used to drink;

Sugar Beach on the west coast (*see p153*)

Blinding white sand at Mont Choisy beach

it is a pretty, white-sand beach shaded by casuarina trees. The clear, shallow water and reef close to shore make it ideal for families and snorkellers.

La Cuvette, a long silky beach with clear water between Grand Baie and Cap Malheureux, is one of the finest spots to swim on the island. It's also one of the best places for sailing, windsurfing and waterskiing.

East coast

The breezier coast, this is the site of some of the island's most exclusive hotels, as well as its most beautiful beaches, such as the 10km (6¼-mile)-long **Belle Mare Plage**. It is good for those who love watersports. In the southeast, **Blue Bay** has the island's best underwater scenery for snorkelling and glass-bottom boat trips. **Île aux Cerfs** is an idyllic

small island close to the coast with powder-white beaches and translucent water on a sand bar. With watersports and watering holes, it makes a great day out. **Île des Deux Cocos** (see p104) is an archetypal island paradise.

West coast

The driest, warmest coast with great sunsets, the flat, shallow beaches of the west tend to suit families with young children. The southwest's **Le Morne Beach and Peninsula** is a favourite with kite-surfers and windsurfers between May and October. **Flic en Flac** is a lively beach resort, with a good range of watersports, boutiques and inexpensive restaurants. The shallow waters are particularly good for young children.

of the distinctively shaped Coin de Mire (Gunner's Quoin), named after the quoin or wedge used under a cannon, looming large beyond the pirogues bobbing in the water.

Cap Malheureux is reached by the coastal road to the right of Grand Baie, by bus, taxi or hire car.

Notre Dame Auxiliatrice. Services: Mon–Fri 1pm, Sat 6pm, Sun 9am.

GRAND BAIE

A small fishing village just 20 years ago, the deep, sheltered cove of Grand Baie

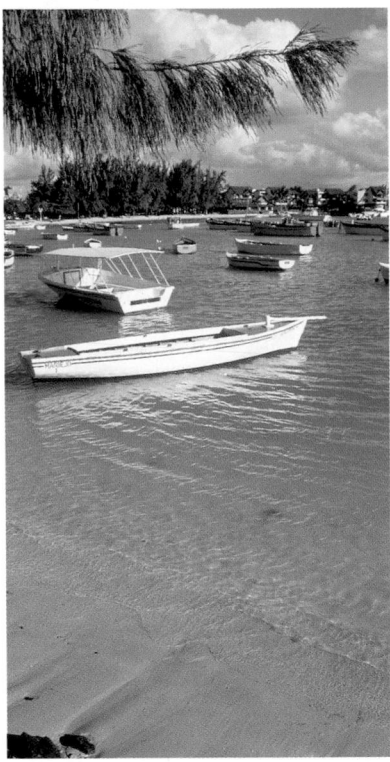

Boats at Grand Baie

GAJAKS

Gajaks is the Creole name for snacks. These are sold from vans in towns, from a glass case on the back of a bicycle, in markets or from makeshift huts alongside public beaches. Safe to eat and surprisingly tasty, they're filling enough for a quick, very cheap lunch.

is now a shopping and leisure paradise, and the heart of the island's nightlife. Bustling and colourful, with a cluster of boutiques, restaurants, bars and discos, it is referred to as Mauritius' little 'St Trop', and attracts those who like some liveliness to go with their beach. Grand Baie is also great for those who want action nearby – there is a range of land and sea excursions as well as every kind of watersport. French cannons can still be seen at Le Canonnier Hotel (*see p151*) at Pointe aux Canonniers or 'Gunner's Point', which sticks out into the sea to the left. The Dutch referred to it as De Vuyle Hoek (Filthy Corner) as many ships sank on its reefs.

The M2 from the airport ends at Grand Baie. It can be reached by bus, taxi or hire car.

NORTHERN EXCURSIONS

Watersports, underwater sports and the Northern Islands all lie nearby, as well as eco-adventures.

Cycling, Yemaya Adventures

See pp104–5.

Coin de Mire or Gunner's Quoin

Horse riding at Mont Choisy Sugar Estate

Fifteen horses live at these stables, which are conveniently situated near Grand Baie. The 1½-hour guided rides through this 1,700ha (4,200-acre) private deer park go past the remains of the old sugar factory and lime kilns and the estate's colonial home. Groups of up to eight are led by an ex-professional racing jockey.
Mont Choisy Sugar Estate, Grand Baie. Tel: 265 6159. Email: info@montchoisy. com. Rides at: 8am & 3pm. Excursion charge. Drive or take a taxi here from Grand Baie.

Kayaking around Île d'Ambre (Amber Island)

See p102.

Northern Islands cruise

Of the six main islands off the north coast, only Île Plate (Flat Island), Îlot Gabriel (Gabriel Island) and Île d'Ambre (Amber Island) can be visited, typically on a day trip from Grand Baie either by catamaran or speedboat.

Trips pass the dramatic cliff face of the wedge-shaped Coin de Mire (Gunner's Quoin), where the beautiful white Paille-en-queue (straw in the tail) bird nests. Catamaran trips land on

Gabriel Island. Nearby Flat Island is now off-limits, to protect its wildlife. Day trips include swimming and snorkelling and a barbecue lunch on board.

Cruise companies line Grand Baie's Coastal Road and Sunset Boulevard, and include: Croisières Australes (*Coastal Road, Grand Baie. Tel: 263 1669. www.croisieres-australes.mu. Excursion charge*).

Île Ronde (Round Island)

Around 375ha (927 acres), Round Island is closed to visitors while the Mauritius Wildlife Foundation (MWF) works to restore the balance of nature

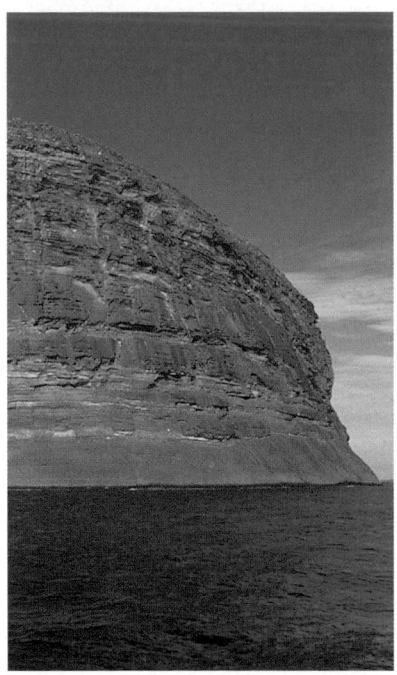

Stunning rock formation in the Northern Islands

on Mauritius' most important ecological site. It is the only place to find the island's remaining endemic reptiles, three unique species of palm tree and the only site in the Indian Ocean where the Petrel bird nests. Round Island's Burrowing Boa, exhibited in the Natural History Museum in Port Louis (*see p31*), is probably now extinct; otherwise it would be the rarest snake in the world.

Underwater adventures

For a taste of Mauritius underwater, without having to get wet, or go deep, climb aboard *Le Nessée*, a semi-submersible glass-bottom boat that heads out from Grand Baie. Fish swim right up to the glass surrounds. *Centre Sport Nautique, Sunset Boulevard, Grand Baie. Tel: 263 8017. www.centrenautique.com. Boat departs: 10am, 12.30pm & 2.30pm. Excursion lasts 1½ hours with snorkelling. Excursion charge.*

Blue Safari Submarine

The only company in the Indian Ocean to offer trips on a semi-submersible scooter of the deep. With two per scooter, passengers must be aged over 12 to ride and over 16 to drive; trips last two hours and can be tailor-made. Its main offering, though, is a 50-minute trip in an air-conditioned submarine down to 35m (115ft), past a wide variety of marine creatures – clownfish, and sometimes turtles, sting rays and sharks

Try an underwater safari while you're in Grand Baie

– and an 18th-century shipwreck. Ask for a space in the submarine that holds five passengers – it is one of only two in the world to have floor-to-ceiling glass surrounds rather than portholes.
Royal Road, Grand Baie. Tel: 263 3333. www.blue-safari.com. Open: daily 8.30am–3.30pm (winter); 7.30am–4.30pm (summer). Trips take 2 hours with transfers. Book well in advance. Excursion charge. Parking behind hotel PLM Azur, Mont Choisy beach.

Solar Sea Walk
The closest to diving that a non-diver can get. Weighed down with a lead belt around your waist and a 40kg (88lb) helmet on your head, sink 3m (10ft) underwater and walk along the seabed amid coral gardens as swirls of colourful fish swim around you (they're being fed!). It's all powered by solar energy. You can catch the moment on a DVD, at an extra charge.
Solar Sea Walk, Coastal Road, Grand Baie. Tel: 263 7819. www.solarseawalk.net. Departures: Mon–Sat 9am, then every 1½ hours until 3pm (last departure). Closed Sun. Boat pickup in central Grand Baie to transport to a platform in the sea; allow 90 minutes (20–25 minutes underwater). Excursion charge; book at least 24 hrs in advance.

NORTHERN ATTRACTIONS

Inland are the graceful Pamplemousses Botanical Gardens, the island's most visited attraction, and its most modern museum, L'Aventure du Sucre, which gives an insight into the island's fascinating history. Domaine Les Pailles, the most accessible Domaine, also lies in the north, providing natural beauty and adventure beyond the beaches.

L'Aventure du Sucre

This vast, ancient sugar mill houses an interactive, modern 5,000sq m (53,800sq ft) exhibition that traces the history of Mauritius. Opened in 2002 in the former Beau Plan sugar factory, imaginative and entertaining media such as film, DVDs and holographic images are used to tell the story of sugar through the ages, with details on the cane plant, manufacturing process, and sugar routes and markets around the world. There are fascinating exhibitions on the slave trade, indentured labourers and colonial houses as well as temporary exhibitions. Children are led through a presentation and quiz by Raj, the Mynah bird, and Floryse, the mongoose. The well-restored machinery is a work of art itself, a mirror reveals the tall chimney, and visitors can walk past the huge vats where sugar was once processed.

You can sample the 15 types of unrefined sugar, served with rum in the Village Boutik. Packaged with other locally made products, these make tasteful gifts. The museum's restaurant, Le Fangourin, under flamboyant trees, serves a lunch of Seychellois fish, Creole and regional dishes as well as tea and pastries.

Beau Plan, Pamplemousses. Just 15 minutes' drive from Port Louis, 0.5km (1/3 mile) from Pamplemousses Botanical Gardens, parking on site. Tel: 243 7900. www.aventuredusucre.com. Open: daily 9am–5pm. Admission charge.

Take a tour of Domaine Les Pailles by horse and carriage

Château Labourdonnais

The newest colonial attraction on the island is this beautiful château set among orchards of tropical fruit trees and perfumed exotic flowers. If you have time, you can hike or mountain bike through the orchards.

Mapou, Rivière du Rempart. Tel: 266 9533. www. unchateaudanslanature.com. Open: daily 9am–5pm. Admission charge.

Domaine Les Pailles

Ten minutes' drive southwest of Port Louis is a 1,500ha (3,700-acre) nature park at the foot of the pretty Moka range. The most commercial of the Domaines, it offers a gentle taste of history, culture and nature. There's plenty to do, including a swimming pool and mini-golf, making it particularly suitable for families. Tour the estate by the train *Lady Alice* or by horse-drawn carriage, or take guided horse rides (*daily 9–11am & 2–5pm*). Other tours include a working replica of an 18th-century ox-powered sugar mill, a functioning rum and essential-oil distillery, and the spice garden. It has a choice of four restaurants for lunch and evening meals. There's a jazz club and

A statue at the Maheswarnath temple

casino here as well as Sega performances that everyone is welcome to see when groups are visiting.

Les Guibies, Pailles. Tel: 286 4225. www.domainelespailles.net (French only). Open: daily 9.30am–5pm. A ten-minute taxi ride from Port Louis.

Maheswarnath temple, Triolet

Maheswarnath was a lucky man, stumbling upon pirate treasure as he worked the fields around Triolet town. In 1857, with his wealth he built this Hindu temple, the largest on the island, in honour of the gods Shiva, Krishna, Vishnu, Muruga, Brahma and Ganesh. The design of old temples is far less lurid and ornate than the new ones, and this one is largely white with a few paintings and designs in traditional colours. The statues are perhaps

TRIOLET

Triolet's claim to fame is that it is the longest town on the island. It has a host of traditional shops and is an atmospheric place to visit during religious festivals such as Diwali and Maha Shivaratree, when everyone takes to the streets.

prettiest, with stone carvings of a bull and horse out front and a wooden tiger guarding the temple entrance.

Triolet Village. Just inland from Trou aux Biches. Open: daily 6am, all candles lit by lunchtime. Donation accepted. Can be reached by hire car, bus or taxi.

Mauritius Aquarium

An attraction for families in the north, the Mauritius Aquarium houses colourful fish found around the island in its five buildings, as well as aquatic creatures such as turtles and octopus (and sharks!). It also has a touch pool encouraging young children to interact with the fish – ideal for those too young to snorkel – and a giant predator tank with scorpion fish and rays.

Royal palms at the Pamplemousses Botanical Gardens

Coastal Road, Pointe aux Piments. Tel: 261 4561. www.mauritiusaquarium.com. Open: Mon–Sat 9.30am–5pm, Sun 10am–4pm; fish feeding daily at 11am. Admission charge.

Sir Seewoosagur Ramgoolam Botanical Gardens/ Pamplemousses Botanical Gardens

What started off as the vegetable garden of Mahé de Labourdonnais is now the third-oldest botanical gardens in the world and one of the most visited sites in Mauritius. Created by French botanist Pierre Poivre as the governor's private garden in the 18th century, it has a huge collection of indigenous and exotic plants from around the world. The governor's bust can be seen opposite the impressive pond full of giant Amazon lilies.

Once covering 100ha (250 acres), today the 20ha (50-acre) garden of ponds and tree-lined avenues contains 600 trees, including one brought by Captain Cook, the curious bleeding tree and a 250-year-old 'Buddha Tree'. Of the 85 species of palm included here, the Talipot palm from Sri Lanka blooms with millions of white and purple flowers once every 30 to 100 years, and then dies. The last bloom was in 2008. There is also a spice garden, deer and a colony of giant tortoises in an enclosure for children.

Make time to shop at **Saga Duty-free Shopping** (*Tel: 243 9900. Open: Mon–Sat 9am–5.30pm, Sun 9am–1pm*),

A guide will explain all the things you can see in the Botanical Gardens

a collection of 20 boutiques opposite the main entrance to Pamplemousses Botanical Gardens that sells crafts, clothes, jewellery, ship models, silk and more. There's also a café and money-changing facility here.

Mahé de Labourdonnais' colonial mansion, Château Mon Plaisir, which in 1768 became the home of Pierre Poivre and overlooks the garden, can also be visited, as can an old sugar mill. Although entrance to the gardens is free, it's good value to hire a guide to walk you through the lovely avenues, named after governors and botanists who lived on the island, smelling camphor and clove leaves and bringing the plants alive.

Royal Road, Pamplemousses. 11km (7 miles) from Port Louis; car park at the main and side entrance.
Tel: 243 9403. Email: ssrbg@intnet.mu.
Open: daily 8.30am–5.30pm.
Free admission.

PIERRE POIVRE (1719–86)

Naturalist Pierre Poivre was born and died in Lyon, France. Selected by the East India Company to seize the monopoly of the spice trade from the Dutch, he brought nutmeg and clove trees aboard Labourdonnais' frigate from Pondicherry in India. Administrator of Île de France from 1749 to 1772, he continued and completed the importation of spice trees to Mauritius. His most famous achievement was the creation of Labourdonnais' garden at Pamplemousses.

Walk: Le Pouce to Port Louis

The third-highest mountain on Mauritius at 812m (2,664ft), Le Pouce or 'The Thumb' is the mountain that most people climb. It's possible to do the return walk in a couple of hours, but going one way to Port Louis makes this walk more interesting, although you'll need a taxi. Take waterproofs, shoes with a good grip and a picnic lunch.

The walk covers a distance of about 9km (5½ miles) and will take about 4 hours.

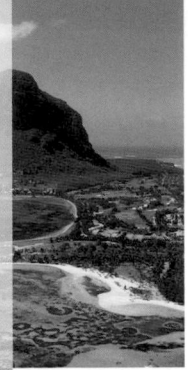

At Moka, turn left at the roundabout towards Mount Ory. After a few kilometres, Le Pouce is signed on the right. After 3km (2 miles), in the village

of La Laura, the road bends sharply to the right. Pull in at a dirt road on the left 25m (27yds) after it (GPS Waypoint no 15, South 20 degrees 12.263).

Keeping Pieter Both Mountain on the right, and Le Pouce ahead, follow the road through the sugar cane, bearing left as the path forks and then narrows. Continue winding around the outer edge of the mountain until after about 2km (1¼ miles) you reach a junction. Take the furthest right of the grassy paths heading up the hill close to the trees, to a cliff-edge viewpoint.

1 Pieter Both Lookout

People often choose to picnic overlooking the distinctive shape and velvety folds of Pieter Both, and so it's the most likely place to spot Macaque monkeys. From here, it's easy to make out the unmistakable thumb shape of Le Pouce on the left.

Walk inland from the ledge to join one of the grassy paths heading right to Le Pouce. Pass through a section of

The foothills of Le Pouce

indigenous forest mixed with exotic trees before climbing the last steep few metres to the top.

2 Le Pouce

From the rocky top, there's a great 360-degree view of most of the island's mountains – as far as Le Morne in the south and, on a clear day, the Northern Islands to Round Island and the best view of Port Louis.

Double back to Le Pouce Junction and turn right, winding around the mountain.

3 Port Louis Viewpoint

With Snail Rock to the left (again named after its shape) and through the trees, Port Louis looks surreal from here.

Continue straight down the path as it gets rocky and narrow and plunges in and out of thicket for about 2km

(1¹⁄₄ miles). When you reach a grassy crossroads at the bottom, turn right and walk on a wide path through an avenue of eucalyptus trees.

4 Le Dauguet Promenade de Santé (Health Walk)

Ebony, mahogany and olive trees can be seen on this walk. Before the government bought the land in 1881, the owner supplied Port Louis with water.

Continue straight until you reach the car park, which closes at 6pm.

5 Port Louis Racecourse

The car park overlooks the historic Champ de Mars racecourse, the oldest in the southern hemisphere and very busy on race days.

From here, wind your way down the hill into Port Louis.

The west

Nicknamed 'the sunset coast', west Mauritius is best known for its family-friendly beaches. It's also the epicentre for big-game fishing, diving, dolphins and the only place for a spot of surfing. However, with a sanctuary for rare birds, markets for bargain-hunting, one of the best examples of colonial architecture and adventure in a vast African-style savanna, this side of the island has more than just seaside to offer.

Large Town
Small Town
POI
Motorway
Main Road
Minor Road

N

Domaine Les Pailles
Eureka
Moka
A7
Quartier Militaire
A3
M2
Corps du Garde 780
Quatre Bornes
Flic en Flac
Phoenix
B2
Trois Mamelles 629
Mt du Rempart 545
Floréal
Curepipe
Casela Nature and Leisure Park & Yemen Nature Escapade
Domaine des Aubinéaux
Tamarin Bay
Tamarin
Henrietta
Trou aux Cerfs
Midlands
Banane
Grande Rivière Noire
Tamarin Mt 548
Tamarin Falls Reservoir
Domaine de Lagrave
Mt Brise Fer 622
Black River
Mare aux Vacoas
Domaine des 7 Vallées
Petite Rivière Noire
Black River Gorges National Park
Grand Bassin
Grand Bois
A10
Île aux Bénitiers
Chamarel
Black River Peak 828
Bois Chéri Tea Factory
Domaine Louisa
Mt Cocotte 771
Le Morne Brabant 555
Chamarel Falls
Bassin Blanc
Piton Savanne 704
A9
B9
Baie du Cap
Frederica Nature Reserve
Chazal
Rivière des Anguilles
B8
St Martin
Bel Ombre
Lot Sancho
St Aubin
La Roche qui Pleure
0 3km
0 2 miles
Souillac
Gris Gris

The classic colonial architecture of Eureka

MOKA
Eureka

One of the most interesting, well-preserved and striking examples of colonial architecture, Eureka lies in a peaceful but powerful setting, between the Moka Mountains and a deep, forested valley. Purpose-built by a British man, Mr Carr, in 1836 to adapt to the tropical climate, it passed through the hands of the island's biggest sugar baron before being rescued from the bulldozer by the present Franco-Mauritian owner.

Eureka is a feat of engineering with its 1,000sq m (10,760sq ft) of wood protected from cyclones and the tropical heat by a wrap-around veranda and blinds, and 109 doors to keep cool. Also typical and particularly pretty here are the turreted windows in its roof, best seen from the back of the house. The 14 rooms house antique furniture made from mahogany and ebony. The baby grand, gramophone and marble stand-alone bath evoke a good

impression of life as it was. Pierre Poivre (*see p43*), who designed Pamplemousses Botanical Gardens, lived next door, and the house boasts visits from British royals.

A traditional Creole lunch is cooked on request in the old stone kitchen decorated with utensils from the 1800s, where cooking demonstrations are given. Gourmet French cuisine with a Creole touch is served in the evening in a beautiful dining room. At the entrance is a small shop selling tasteful gifts and rum as well as fruits grown here. Walk for 15 minutes down a narrow dirt path among ebony trees and bamboo to come to four waterfalls on the Moka River and a tempting natural swimming pool and jacuzzi cut out of the rock.

Eureka, Moka. Tel: 433 8477. Book in advance. www.maisoneureka.com. Most people come on an excursion, but you can arrive by taxi or hire car. Open: Mon–Sat 9am–5pm & Sun 9am–3pm. Admission charge for guided tours; lunch extra.

CUREPIPE AND ENVIRONS

Curepipe, at 500m (1,640ft), is the island's highest town, and locally known as the rainiest (with 3m/10ft per year). Thought to have got its name from being the place where French soldiers on a long march would stop and clean or 'cure' their pipes, it has a few attractive colonial buildings such as the town hall. Mark Twain may have called it 'the nastiest spot on earth', but visitors seem to like it. The main reasons to come here are to shop at centres such as **Garden Village** (*21 Sir Winston Churchill Street. Tel: 675 0321*). Take a quick spin around Trou aux Cerfs, and visit the Floréal Textile

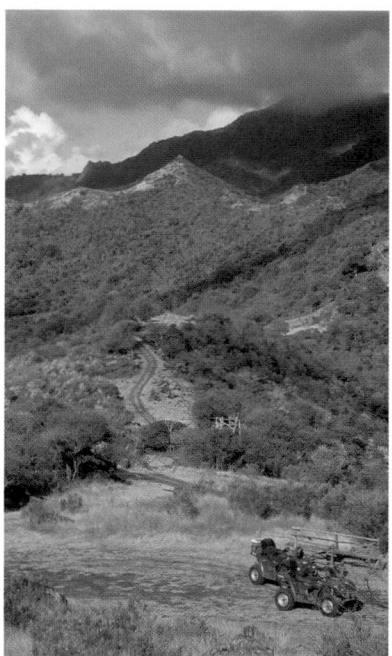

Quad biking in Casela Yemen

MARE AUX VACOAS

Mare aux Vacoas reservoir is the island's largest lake. Surrounded by pines, it lies 600m (2,000ft) above sea level and is a pretty stop to admire the view on the way from Curepipe to Chamarel.

Museum nearby (*see pp52–3*). Curepipe is easier visited on an excursion as attractions are not well signed; even taxi drivers get lost here.

Casela Nature and Leisure Park

Nestled in the lush vegetation of the Rivière Noire district, Casela Nature and Leisure Park is a sanctuary for rare birds with 140 species of birds from 5 continents of the world. Its 90 aviaries on 25ha (61 acres) of land house around 1,500 feathered friends, a variety of mammals and a petting farm for children. The star attraction is the pink pigeon, the cousin of the dodo, saved from extinction. The park serves a simple Creole lunch under thatch if booked in advance. Although not a terribly inspiring layout, it is one of few such attractions for families.
Casela Nature and Leisure Park, Cascavelle. Tel: 727 6076. www.caselayemen.mu. Open: daily May–Sept 9am–5pm; Oct–Apr daily 9am–6pm. Admission charge. A 10-minute taxi ride inland from Flic en Flac.

Casela Yemen Nature Escapade

Under the same umbrella as Casela Nature and Leisure Park, but next door and on the third-biggest sugar

More colonial architecture in Curepipe – this time at Garden Village Shopping Centre

estate in Mauritius, Yemen has 4,500ha (11,120 acres) of hills, valleys and grassy savanna, and you feel as if you could be in Africa. Antelopes, zebra, ostrich and even a giraffe can be seen along with some 9,000 free-roaming deer on a quad safari (*9am, 12.30pm & 2.30pm daily*). A lion encounter (*9am, 10.30am, 2pm & 3.30pm daily*) will thrill children (over 1.5m/5ft) as well as a 45-minute mini-safari by open bus (*every hour 9.30am–3.30pm*). Randofun is a day's adventure with hiking, Nepalese bridges, zipline, barbecue and swim through a canyon, for 8 years and up (*9am–3pm daily*).

Guided adventures include hiking, off-road double-quad, segway (two-wheeled vehicle), buggies and 4WD rides through 300km (186 miles) of track up and down hills and a half-day quad, swim and zipline. Wild boar, giant fruit bats, monkeys and moorhens can be seen, and some ebony and teak trees. *See previous entry for contact details.*

Dolphin Catamaran Cruise, Tamarin Bay

Named after the Tamarind trees the Dutch planted here, a highlight of this area is a catamaran cruise in Tamarin

(*Cont. on p52*)

Colonial houses

Most colonial architecture seen on Mauritius was brought by the French when they settled on the island in 1715, and it became a blueprint for building by the local population. Cyclones, in particular Cyclone Carol in the 1960s, claimed many houses, and many local people rebuilt in concrete. A national heritage fund was set up in 2003 to preserve the remaining historic buildings.

The French adapted their building style to the tropics, and a number of the plantation homes dating from the 18th and 19th centuries have survived. Although many are still private homes, glimpsed through the sugar cane, some have been converted into elegant restaurants and living museums open to the public. Often set in tropical gardens, these are places to experience the refined way of life in the past.

Traditional colonial architecture can be found all around the island. The blue-and-white painted town hall in Curepipe is an attractive remnant of the past, and is open to visitors, as is the Plaza Theatre in Rose Hill, also the largest theatre complex in the Indian Ocean. These two buildings, along with the police station, the old school in Vacoas, the courthouse and post office in Flacq, and what is now the Shelter for Alcoholic Women in Flacq are all good examples of colonial architecture.

Features of colonial houses

Colonial houses were traditionally built of wood, laid on a base to keep them away from the damp ground and for ventilation. Roofs were originally made of *armagasse*, a mixture for tiles that became as hard as marble and resistant to rain. This concealed a vaulted roof (which in houses open to the public now often hosts a museum) that allows air to circulate. Typical features include ornamental turrets, rows of attic

St Aubineaux, Curepipe

The house at Domaine Les Pailles

windows and a roof decorated with lacy wooden or metal fringes, or *lambrequins*, always with a botanical theme. There's always a wide, long *verangue* (veranda), frequently with two gables at the front that could be either open or closed. Eureka (*see p47*) has a wrap-around veranda Clever touches are decorative pierced screens that look pretty, and help keep the house cool and dry, and doors that replace windows – Eureka has 109 doors! Official buildings such as Government House in Port Louis were built out of brick or stone, although still decorated with *lambrequins*. Poorer cottages were made out of hardwood until the 1960s, when many were rebuilt in concrete and painted bright colours, with the veranda generally enclosed to give the family more space.

Inside the colonial mansions, the design was simple. There were no corridors – residents crossed the house through the rooms. The lounge often occupied the whole width of the house, and the kitchen and shower rooms were in a separate building or at the back of the house. The soft blue found on curtains, windows and woodwork inside the house is the Wedgwood blue of the famous English pottery. Walls were whitewashed with local lime, and the addition of permanganate gave the shutters their grey-blue colour.

Five colonial houses to visit
North
Château Labourdonnais, Mapou
Domaine Les Pailles, near Port Louis
Government House, Port Louis
West
Eureka, near Moka
St Aubineaux, Curepipe
Southeast
Le Saint Aubin, Rivière des Anguilles

Bay to see the rare black and long-beak dolphins. Although sometimes boats crowd the dolphins, it is a thrill to see them and some trips allow you to swim with them. Snorkelling and a barbecue lunch on board makes for a relaxing day or half day, and there are great views from the water to Le Morne.

Croisières Australes (Le Morne). Tel: 263 1669. Depart: 9.15am from Le Morne Anglers Club in Black River for a full day on the Harris Wilson Catamaran, arriving back at 3.30pm. The trip watches the dolphins in Tamarin and, after a barbecue lunch, travels to a snorkelling spot. Excursion charge.
Dolswim. Tel: 422 9281.
www.dolswim.com. Excursions leave from the Island Sports Hotel, Black River.
Depart: 8am for 2 hours to swim with the dolphins. Excursion charge.
A dolphin- and whale-watching half day is also offered.

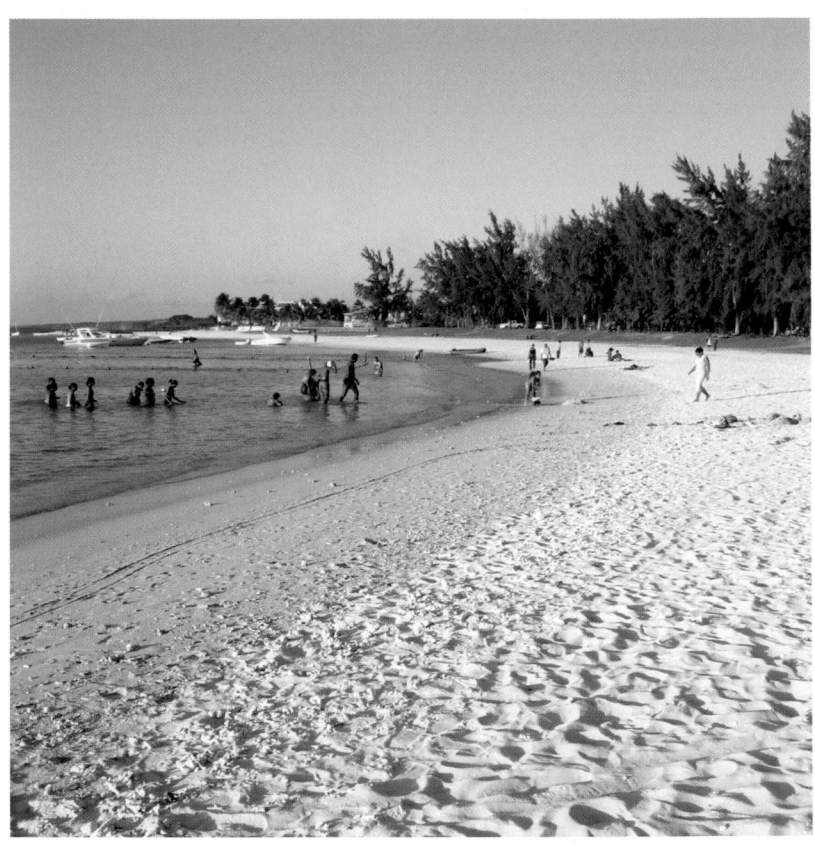

Flic en Flac beach

Flic en Flac

A popular and lively beach resort, Flic en Flac is a good place to catch some local nightlife on summer weekends. Food sellers line the shore, inexpensive restaurants and a disco lie opposite, and you may catch some impromptu Sega music and dancing on the beach. Local tales have it that the name 'Flic en Flac' came from the sound of the French soldiers' boots squelching across the marshes here, serving as a warning to people poaching deer from the plains. The Dutch called it Fried Landt Flaak or Free Flat Land, and this may have been mispronounced by the Creole population.

Floréal

Floréal is known as the textile centre of the island, and has a cluster of 15 boutiques gathered around a garden. However, as a shopping centre it doesn't live up to its hype.
Floréal Square, John Kennedy Street. Boutiques. Tel: 601 1000. Email: floreal-sq@intnet.mu. Open: Mon–Fri 9.30am–5.30pm, Sat 9.30am–4pm. Closed: Sun.
Come by taxi, hire car or excursion.

Tamarin Falls

A series of seven waterfalls with a bathing pool below, Tamarin Falls is about 8km (5 miles) from Curepipe, and a 2km (1¼-mile) walk from the village of Henrietta. It's a difficult hike and not so easy to find, so most people visit on excursions, where a guide is provided for canyoning here.
Excursions or buses from Curepipe or Port Louis, taxi or hire car.

Trou aux Cerfs

Trou aux Cerfs means 'Hole of the Stags', and the lake at the bottom of this 600–700,000-year-old volcanic crater in Curepipe was once their watering hole. Walking the 1km (²/₃ mile) around the rim on the old tarmac road will give you good views over the central plains and the mountains beyond. This is a place to spot local celebs or politicians chinwagging on a stroll or jogging in the morning and late afternoon. An unmarked narrow track, signalled by a break in the bushes and concrete steps, leads 85m (280ft) down to the small lake at the crater's bottom in about 20 minutes; just don't forget the insect repellent.
Drive up or take a taxi from Curepipe (it's not signposted), following John Pope Hennessy Street, and right into Edgar Hughes Street. Parking at the top just before the road is blocked off with a chain. Free admission.

A PLACE IN THE SUN?

Foreigners have been able to buy their own slice of Mauritian paradise since 2006. Luxury villas are available in upmarket resorts such as Villas Valriche (*www.villasvalricheexperience.com*) and more developments are being planned. More affordable villas and apartments can be found at Emerald Heights (*www.emeraldheightsmauritius.com*) near the south coast.

Walk: The Macchabée Trail

This mostly gentle walk heads along a ridge, with great views over the Black River Gorges through gaps in the guava trees. It's a one-way self-guided walk on a well-marked trail and is best arranged with taxi drop-off and pickup at the other end. The trail offers the chance to see rare birds and tall endemic trees, among them ebony. It tends to rain a lot here, so take waterproofs with you, and in summer insect repellent.

The walk covers a distance of 10km (6 miles) and will take 3½ hours.

Start beside the National Park Information sign on the wide dirt vehicle track beside the Petrin Information Centre, step over the chain and continue straight on.

The Black River

1 Endemic trees and plants

The fenced area to your right is where the Mauritius Wildlife Foundation (MWF) has planted endemic trees and plants. A small exhibition and plant samples identified in the garden are found here. This gives a good idea of how different Mauritius looked before humans arrived.

Walk through an avenue of guava hedges until after 1km (²⁄₃ mile), marked by a stone sign, you come to a clearing on your left.

2 View Black River Gorges

Black River Peak, the highest point in Mauritius, rises from the hillsides on your left like a little cap.

Continue straight for 0.5km (¹⁄₃ mile) until another clearing opens on your left-hand side.

3 Waterfalls viewpoint

Two lovely waterfalls cascade down the gorge. Go a little further for an even better view of them and a moody view of the mountains. Wild flowers are found in this forest with some endemic trees. Mud disturbed by the side of the road is a sign of wild pigs.

After 2km (1¹/₄ miles), take the left track signed Macchabée Viewpoint/Black River. After 3km (2 miles), you'll get your first view of the sea, to the right beyond the mountains. After 4km (2¹/₂ miles), the road seems to come to an end at the viewpoint.

4 Gorges viewpoint

A stupendous view of gorges either side, and Tamarin Mountain and the sea in front. The path now descends steps to the right followed by a 1km (²/₃-mile) steep and narrow muddy scramble over roots, hanging on to endemic trees such as ebony, on the way down.

At the crossroads at the bottom, take the right fork down an easy path, through the gates, and zigzag on a grassy then rocky path, through eucalyptus trees. Listen out for the Black River and look out for monkeys and birds.

5 Black River

Named after the rocks in it, there are three tributaries of this river to cross before arriving at the Visitors' Centre along a shady avenue of soaring trees, some endemic. The first requires you to wade over a shallow ford. The second is the prettiest, with trees anchored in the water. It's only a half-hour return walk from the Visitors' Centre to the ford, so this scenic section of the path is often busy. You can swim if you wish. There is more information about birds, plants and the invasion of species at the Visitors' Centre.

Wildlife on Mauritius

As a small, isolated island in the middle of a vast ocean, there was little opportunity for the migration of animals from other continents. The only indigenous mammals were five species of bat, and only one fruit bat survives today, seen in forested areas around the island.

When the dodo was still in existence, Mauritius was inhabited by two species of Giant Tortoise, along with 13 other reptiles of which five are left today, three of which – the Ornate Day gecko, the Keel Scale boa and the Telfair skink – are only found on Round Island. The tortoises were loaded on to ships as live food and, along with the dodo (*see pp8–9*), became extinct by

An Aldabra tortoise at La Vanille

the end of the 17th century. The tortoises seen on Mauritius today were brought by Charles Darwin from Aldabra in 1875, and the island now has the largest breeding programme of Aldabra tortoises in the world at La Vanille Réserve des Mascareignes (*see pp90–91*), where they can be seen at each stage of development. Tortoises have recently been reintroduced to Rodrigues.

The other wildlife you will see on Mauritius is descended from those brought by progressive waves of settlers. The Dutch brought deer from Java (where they are now rare) and pigs (now wild) from Holland. The Portuguese brought the Macaque monkey in 1528 from Malaysia. The *tendrac*, which looks like a hedgehog, and the hump-backed Zebu cattle came from Madagascar.

Birds

In the dodo's time, Mauritius was one of the richest oceanic islands in the biodiversity of its birdlife, but only 9 of its 26 endemic species now remain, all critically endangered. The pink pigeon and the Mauritius kestrel are the most famous. Saved from extinction by the British expatriate Gerald Durrell's

Île aux Aigrettes, home to pink pigeons

Captive Breeding Programme set up in 1973, they are among the rarest birds in the world. The Mauritius kestrel, the island's only bird of prey, was reduced to just two pairs in 1974, but there are now up to 800 in the wild, over half living in the Kestrel Valley (*see pp82–3*). The pink pigeon is Mauritius' largest surviving native bird. There were only 20 left on the island in the early 1970s, but there are now over 360. This bird can be seen in a cage at Casela Nature and Leisure Park (*see p48*), semi-wild on Île aux Aigrettes (*see pp84–5 & p90*) or, if lucky, in the uplands of the Black River Gorges. The Mauritius parakeet, the rarest parrot in the world, was down to only 25 birds in the 1980s, but can now be spotted on walks in the Black River Gorges.

The other six endemic birds are the Mauritius cuckoo-shrike, black bulbul, Paradise flycatcher, grey white-eye, olive white-eye and a song bird, the Mauritius fody, which is now the most endangered of all.

Bird-spotting

All of the birds can be seen in the Black River Gorges National Park (*see pp58–63*), but other good bird-watching spots open to the public include Pointe aux Piments, Bassin Blanc (a natural lake), Macchabée Forest Road, Bel Ombre Nature Reserve, Petite Rivière Noire Saltpans, Tamarin Saltpans, and Domaine d'Anse Jonchée.

The Mauritian Wildlife Foundation (MWF). www.mauritian-wildlife.org

THE SOUTHWEST

The southwest has some of Mauritius' most beautiful and varied natural landscapes. It ranges from the unusual coloured earths of Chamarel to the lush forested Black River Gorges National Park, which houses the island's largest natural lake. Cradling this is the bare rock face of Le Morne Brabant and an untamed stretch of rocky coastline interspersed with traditional fishing villages, once frequented by pirates, where the fishermen still sell their catch from roadside stalls. The first hotels opened here in 2004, along with a golf course and nature park.

HIKING TIPS

Plaine Champagne is green because it rains year-round, so bring waterproofs if hiking here. Slippery paths can be dangerous – bring proper walking shoes or boots with a good grip. In summer, particularly, bring plenty of water and sunblock as well as insect repellent if going deep in the forest. Unlike in many countries, there are no guides hanging around offering their services at the start of trails. For guided walks in the Black River Gorges, contact local trekking specialists.

Black River Gorges National Park

Named after the black stones in the river running through it, this is the only

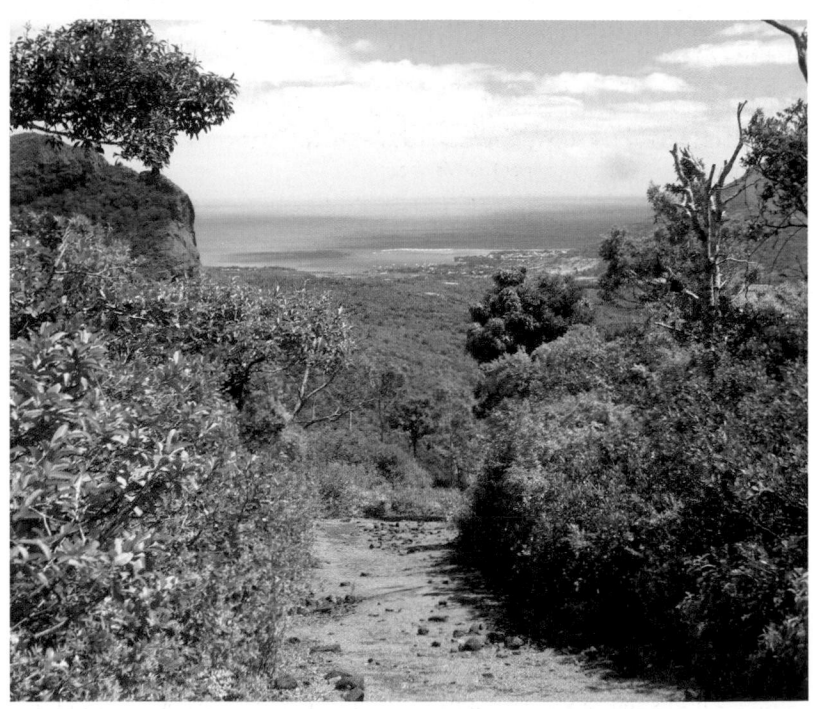

The Macchabée Trail in the Black River Gorges National Park

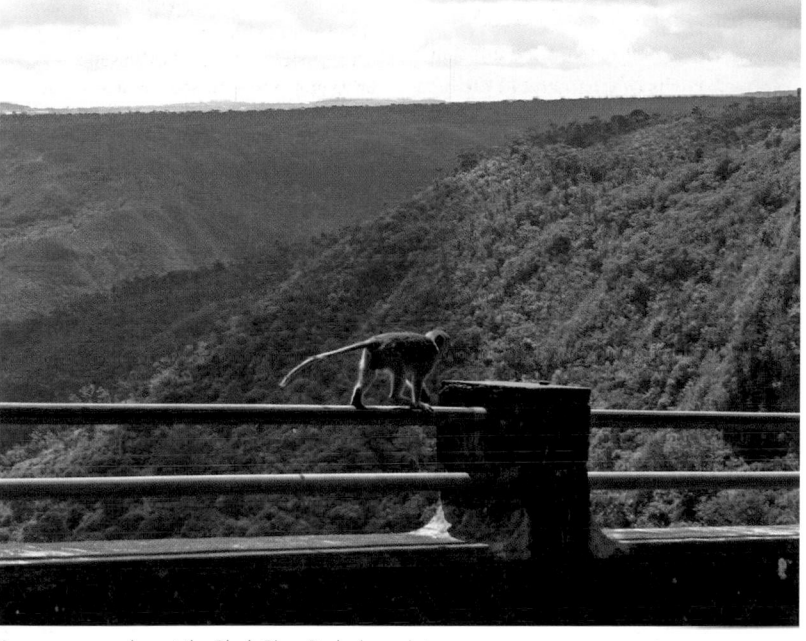

A macaque monkey at the Black River Peak viewpoint

inland national park in Mauritius. It lies upon Plaine Champagne, which is the name of the creamy white flowers of the privet that grows here. These looked, to Mauritian imagination, like the froth on Champagne. The park covers over 6,794ha (16,790 acres), or 3.5 per cent of the country, and has the largest remaining and most accessible native forest on the island. Although invaded by exotic species such as guava and privet, Black River Gorges National Park has the greatest concentration of ebony trees on the island, over 309 species of flowering plants and all 9 of Mauritius' endemic birds. Watch out for the Paille-en-queue (straw in the tail) flying over the tree canopy – this elegant white bird has been adopted as the emblem of Air Mauritius. It is also a good place to spot the Mauritius fruit bat. Look for the umbrella-shaped *bois de natte* tree, characteristic of the island's upland forest and often decorated with orchids, ferns and lichens. Pink pigeons were introduced to the park in 2009.

The top five popular trails in the park are:

Macchabée Trail (10km/6 miles one-way Petrin to Black River Visitors' Centre, leisurely 3½ hours). The most popular walk from here, it starts overlooking the gorge and ends up deep inside it (*see pp54–5*).

Black River Peak (9km/5¹/₂ miles return from Petrin, moderate, leisurely 2 hours). Although much of the walk is in the guava trees, the view at the end, from the highest peak in Mauritius at 828m (2,717ft), is worth it (*see opposite*).

Bel Ombre (18km/11 miles return, 4–5 hours' moderate walk). This has the greatest change in elevation of all the walks, from overlooking the gorges right down to the sea. The lower tropical forest is a good place to spot rare birds and bats.

Cascade des Galets (3km/2 miles return from Alexandra Falls, strenuous). Although short, a good hike down to a pretty 152m (500ft) waterfall.

Parakeet Trail (8km/5 miles one-way from Plaine Champagne to Black River Visitors' Centre, strenuous). Deep in the forest, this is the place to spot rare and endangered birds.

There are two visitor centres in the park, the Petrin Information Centre at the eastern end of the park on the 737m (2,418ft) forested plateau of Plaine Champagne, and the Black River Visitors' Centre at the park's western entrance in the lower gorges, although this is currently closed for renovation (toilets, picnic area and park open). The Petrin Information Centre sells an inexpensive map detailing around 60km (37 miles) of trails throughout the park, varying from shady paths deep in the gorges to the often cloud-shrouded ridge walk to

Black River Peak (*see opposite*); most start near the centre. A nature trail with native plants has been created near the **Petrin Information Centre** – pick up a leaflet identifying what's there.

Petrin Information Centre, Plaine Champagne. Tel: 258 0057. Open: Mon–Fri 9am–3.15pm, closed weekends. Black River Visitors' Centre. Tel: 258 0059. Open: Mon–Fri 9am–5pm, Sat & Sun 9am–5pm.

You'll need a hire car, a taxi or to come as part of an excursion here as, being uninhabited, Plaine Champagne is the only place on the island not served by public transport.

PLANTS OF MAURITIUS

The island is covered with colourful tropical flowers, 60 orchid species alone, and hedges are a riot of bougainvillea. You may also spot yellow alamanda flowers, flame trees, hibiscus, strelitzia, oleanders and poinsettias. Mauritius is the second-largest producer of cut flowers after the Netherlands, and many people buy the dramatic red anthuriums (from the airport) to take home.

Mauritius was once covered in hardwood forest, but these tall, straight trees were exported to Europe by early settlers. When the French arrived in 1715, the land was further cleared for sugar plantations, and today Mauritius has only 1.9 per cent of its natural vegetation remaining, mostly forests clinging to rugged valleys or steep mountain slopes. This natural habitat still supports 700 species of indigenous plants, although with introduced plants competing and animals destroying their fruits and seedlings, many are threatened with extinction.

The best places to see native plants are Pamplemousses Gardens, Île aux Aigrettes and the Black River Gorges National Park.

Alexandra Falls

Although recently landscaped, Alexandra Falls itself is a disappointing trickle. However, it is worth driving the 1km (²/₃ mile) off the main road through a lovely avenue of paper bark trees for the views across the valley to Bel Ombre in the southwest.

Signed on the left 4km (2¹/₂ miles) after the Petrin Information Centre.

Black River Peak viewpoint

One of the most popular viewpoints on the island, this gives great views north over the impressive Black River

GUAVAS

Plaine Champagne teems with local families picking ripe guavas in March and April. Guava jelly and jam are for sale in shops around the island and make a tasty souvenir.

Gorges to the mountains beyond. To the left is the Black River Peak, at 828m (2,717ft) the highest point in Mauritius; opposite, a pretty waterfall tumbles into the gorge. When uncrowded, it's possible to catch sight of Macaque monkeys cavorting along the railings.

5km (3 miles) past the Petrin Information Centre, on your right.

Bougainvillea is a common sight in the hedgerows

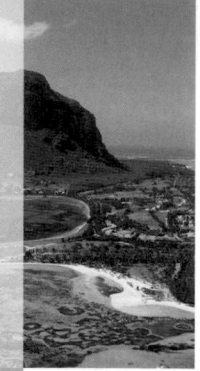

Walks: Cascades 500 Pieds and Black River Peak

These are two contrasting walks in the Black River Gorges National Park, on Plaine Champagne. The Cascades 500 Pieds follows the river down to one of the most beautiful, but off the beaten track, waterfalls on the island. Take waterproofs, shoes with a good grip, and insect repellent. The Black River Peak walk is rewarded with a unique view from the highest peak in Mauritius.

CASCADES 500 PIEDS WALK

The walk covers a distance of 3km (2 miles) and takes a leisurely 1½ hours. It is a short but more challenging hike than Black River Peak on a narrow, sometimes rocky, path. Drive to Alexandra Falls through a lovely avenue of paper bark trees to start this walk.

1 Alexandra Falls

Recently landscaped, there are paths, picnic tables, and a bridge leading to a viewpoint with an outlook across the valley to the sea near Bel Ombre in the south, and these small falls to the left. *Walk to the left of the small bridge to the top of the falls and cross on the stepping*

stones over the small river. Follow the narrow path at the other side as it twists down the left-hand side of the river.

2 Look and listen

The path opens out in places to give excellent views, and small streams crisscross it. Stop and listen to the birds and the distant sound of the river.
Continue for about half an hour to reach the falls.

3 Cascades 500 Pieds

On the right-hand side of the falls, which tumble down 152m (500ft), carefully crawl forward to look over a cliff face. It is difficult to photograph, so take in what you see and remember.
Retrace your steps back to the car park.

BLACK RIVER PEAK WALK

The walk covers a distance of 9km (5½ miles) and takes 3 hours. It is a popular, easy return walk on a well-worn roomy trail along the forested ridge, gentle enough for the family.

To start the walk, park the car, if driving, at the Black River Peak car park. It's then a short distance along the road to the start of the clearly marked footpath.

1 Black River Peak viewpoint

This faces north over the gorge and beyond to many of Mauritius' mountains, making it one of the most popular viewpoints on the island. Picnic tables and vans selling drinks and snacks make it a good place to begin and end the walk.

The gently undulating path passes through a forest of mainly leafy green privet and guava, too thick and high to see any views but with just enough roots and rocks to make it interesting.

2 Almost there

Just before reaching the peak, there is a clearing and a steep walk uphill that seems as though you've made it. But continue on.
Walk another 10 minutes, and scramble up rocks at the end to reach the top of the peak.

3 Black River Peak

You're rewarded with a unique view of the southwest coast, including Le Morne Brabant, Chamarel, Île aux Bénitiers and Tamarin Mountain.
Return the way you came.

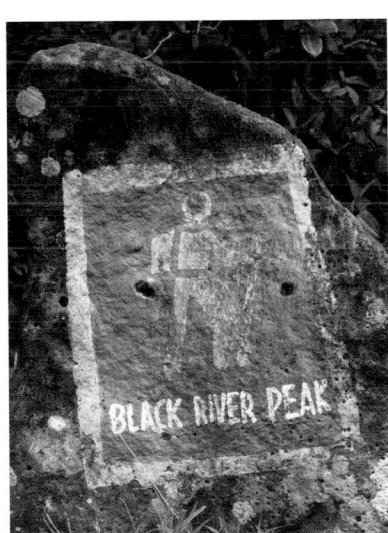

Entrance to the Black River Peak walk

The strange Coloured Earth at Chamarel

Baie du Cap

It's the dramatic road winding beside pristine bays before travelling under rocky overhangs and past lush hillsides around the river just before Baie du Cap that makes this place memorable.

MATTHEW FLINDERS

Returning home after a two-year voyage of discovery in 1803, British explorer Matthew Flinders stopped off at Baie du Cap only to be arrested and detained as a spy for six years by the French governor. Flinders is most famous for mapping the coastline of Australia. His book, *A Voyage to Terra Australis*, was published in 1814, just a day before he died.

Climb on to the rocky outcrop at the river mouth for the best view of one of the most dramatic roads on the coast. The contemporary Matthew Flinders Memorial, sculpted out of copper, lies just after it. Before the road was built around the river in 1930, couples had to wade across to marry at the chapel on the other side.

Approach from Le Morne to get the best views (see p69). Park at the Matthew Flinders Memorial to explore the area.

Chamarel

Here, nature has conspired to produce seven coloured furrows of volcanic

PIRATE LIFE

The small rocky island of Îlot Sancho in Baie du Jacotet near Bel Ombre has a ship's anchor embedded in the coral, a possible treasure sign left by pirates. There is evidence of past pirate activity on the other side of the present main road – piles of coral, fired to make it more resistant to weathering. Is treasure still here, buried beneath the sugar cane?

semi-traditional Le Chamarel Restaurant (*see p155*) is the easiest place to buy some to take home. It usually attracts the crowds for its great view over Île aux Bénitiers and Le Morne. *Main Road, Chamarel. Tel: 483 8298 or 623 5068. Open: daily 7am–5.30pm. Admission charge. Many excursions come here, otherwise by local bus, hire car or taxi.*

ash in bizarre shades of pink, purple, orange and grey. Caused by oxygenation of minerals, no matter how much the earth moves they always settle back into separate colours – proved by mixing the earth in a test tube. The dramatic **Chamarel Falls**, plunging 100m (328ft) over a cliff ledge, are the island's highest. Some people may find this more impressive than the Coloured Earth, a short walk away, viewed from a wooden platform and best seen in the late afternoon. Still, curiosity and the promise of a lunch at one of the rustic table d'hôte restaurants in Chamarel village, 4km (2½ miles) away, lures most people here. Mainly populated by Creole villages, Chamarel was named after Antoine Regis Chazal de Chamarel, a French army captain who farmed vanilla, pepper and coffee.

Chamarel is one of the few places in Mauritius with restaurants serving home-cooked Mauritian dishes such as octopus vindaloo, many in unpretentious surroundings. It is also famous for its coffee. The open-sided

Chazal

Chazal is the only zipline (death slide) adventure park in the Indian Ocean. Here, 11 speed ziplines criss-cross for 2km (1¼ miles) over the treetops and above the pretty Rivière des Galets in Chamonix. The highest zipline is at 40m

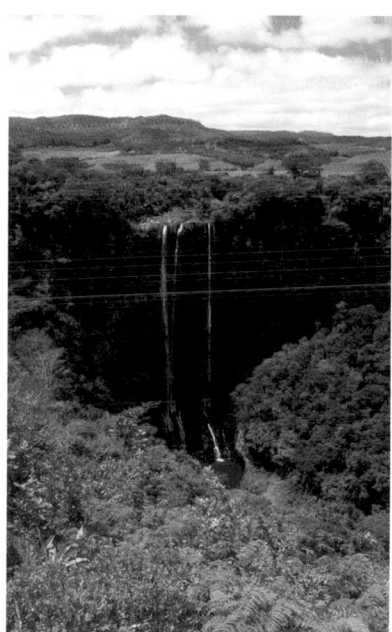

Chamarel Falls, Mauritius' highest waterfall

Flying through the trees at Chazal

(131ft), the lowest 3m (10ft), the longest 160m (524ft) and the shortest 25m (82ft), and the experience lasts for three or four hours. It includes cooling off in a pool at the base of a waterfall and a table d'hôte lunch such as rice, curry and paratha. Groups are of no more than 15 at a time and children 4 years and older are welcome. Hooked up by a harness, it's designed to be relaxing, with little walking in between. The guides are well trained by a Via Ferrata expert. A nine-target archery course is also offered, with compact bows, in a clearing in the forest. River trekking and easy canyoning are also available here.

Chamonix. Hire a car or take a taxi; follow the yellow arrows off-road until you reach a car park. Tel: 622 7234 or 422 3117/3120 (mobile).
Activities: daily 8.30am and 12.30pm. Book in advance.
Admission charge.

TASTE THE ISLAND'S TIPPLE

Sip on high-quality rum at the Rhumerie de Chamarel distillery. Lunch can also be enjoyed at L'Alchimiste à la carte restaurant on the plantation.
Route Royale. Tel: 483 7980. www. rhumeriedechamarel.com. Open: Mon–Sat 9.30am–5.30pm. Closed: Sun.

Frederica Nature Reserve can be visited by helicopter

Frederica Nature Reserve, Domaine de Bel Ombre

This well-kept 1,012ha (2,500-acre) nature reserve lies in Bel Ombre adjacent to the Black River Gorges National Park and just opposite the hotels on the southwest coast.

Bel Ombre means 'Beautiful Shadows', and the restored sugar factory from this estate lies at the entrance to the hotels along the wild and desolate, but inviting, beach there.

Rent double-seater quad bikes or go on a 4WD journey from the house with the bright yellow shutters for a three-hour trip into the plains, where deer, monkeys and wild boar roam, and there is a stunning 152m (500ft) waterfall in the forest. Otherwise, a minimum of six is needed to trek into the undulating hills. A good-value 'prix fixe' lunch is available afterwards at the Golf Club restaurant if Le Château

Restaurant, in a building dating back to the early 1800s, is still closed for renovation.

Domaine de Bel Ombre.
Tel: 623 5615/729 4498 (mobile).
www.domainedebelombre.mu.
Quad and 4WD: daily 9.30am–12.30pm & 1.30–4.30pm.
Trekking: daily 9am–noon. Book in advance for activities and restaurant. Admission charge. Taxi, helicopter, hire car or local bus, or if staying nearby, by foot.

CASUARINAS

Much of Mauritius' coast is bordered by Australian native casuarina (*filao*) trees planted in the 1930s. These look attractive, but leave the sandy soil acidic and unsuitable for other vegetation, and they drop sharp cones that litter the beaches. Since 2001, however, they have gradually been replaced by endemic coastal trees.

Grand Bassin

One of only two natural lakes in Mauritius, Grand Bassin, in the crater of an extinct volcano on Plaine Champagne, is Mauritian Hindus' most sacred site. It's known as Ganga Talao (Lake of the Ganges) locally, and Hindus believe it sprang from drops of water from the holy River Ganges in India. In 1972, sacred water from the Ganges was poured into it and candy-coloured shrines and temples built on its banks. As a pilgrimage site for thousands of Mauritian Hindus, who walk here during the Maha Shivaratree

THE *TREVESSA*

When the British steamer the *Trevessa* sank in 1923 almost 3,000km (2,000 miles) from Mauritius, it seemed unlikely that there would be any survivors. However, 16 men survived 25 days at sea in a lifeboat which eventually landed at St Martin, near Bel Ombre. A monument marking the event lies near the old quay.

festival or 'the great night of Shiva', it is best visited during a festival (*see p18*). Nevertheless, on any day devotees can be seen lighting incense in coconut shells and leaving offerings of fruit and

Two-seater quad bikes at Frederica Nature Reserve

A pink Hindu temple at Grand Bassin

century. In 2008, it was declared a UNESCO World Heritage Site. It forms the backdrop to a row of quiet luxury hotels and an alluring 4km (2½-mile) beach. The mountain is a challenging climb (*see p71*) and the beach is said to be one of the best places for kite-surfing in the world (*see p135*).

To reach Le Morne Brabant, take the B9 around the south coast.

Parc Aventure, Domaine Louisa

An army-style challenging obstacle course through a 12ha (30-acre) forest shaded by a hill. This is a clamber along a series of rope bridges and nets, balancing along swinging logs through the trees. It should take around two and a half hours if the adventure track is also included, flying through the forest on ziplines. After exertions, lunch is offered (brought here from Chamarel Restaurant nearby – *see p155*).

Domaine Louisa. About 2km (1¼ miles) from Chamarel Coloured Earth. Tel: 234 5385. www.parc-aventure-chamarel.com. Open: daily 9.30am–4pm. Bookings only. Children aged 6 years and up (but best aged 12 and up). Bring insect repellent. Admission charge.

flowers on the many platforms around the lake. The newest addition is a Shiva statue, 33m (108ft) high to represent Shiva's 108 names. You can visit independently to see the Shiva Lingham, the burning throat of Shiva symbolised by a stone, and stroll up to the Hanuman (the monkey god) temple, but a tour will bring the Hindu mythology alive, as there is no written explanation.

Le Morne Brabant

Referred to as Le Morne for short, this bare, rocky mountain is Mauritius' mini-answer to South Africa's table-top mountain with its completely flat top. In a remote part of the island, not too far from the first settlement in the southeast, this is where runaway slaves lived and hid in caves in the 19th

---

TRUTH OR LEGEND?

When British soldiers approached Le Morne in 1835 to tell the slaves they were free men, the slaves threw themselves off the top, rather than face recapture. Whether truth or legend, it gave this mountain its name which means 'The Mournful'.

Climbing the mountains of Mauritius

Part of what makes Mauritius special is its mountains. Unusual and dramatic shapes poke out around the island, giving it a moody feel. Myths and legends are associated with some mountains; others breathe stories of Mauritius' past. Although you won't see it on your hotel tour list, all can be trekked and climbed.

These treks range from an easy three-hour walk up Le Pouce (*see pp44–5*) or Black River Peak (*see p63*), both suitable for families, to climbing the precarious-looking boulder atop Pieter Both or ziplining across a 450m (1,476ft) drop at the top of the bare rock face of Le Morne Brabant on the far reaches of the southwest coast. For most mountain climbing here, a guide is recommended. Some mountains, such as Le Morne, are on private property so permission needs to be obtained before climbing them. Many trails aren't well worn or marked, so it's easy to get lost, and the climbs are often technical in parts and sometimes slippery.

The three mountain ranges of Mauritius include: the Moka Range,

distinguished by its unusual shapes and stretching 20km (12½ miles) around Port Louis, from Mount Ory to Nouvelle Découverte; the Black River Chain, which reaches from Mount du Rempart just below Quatre Bornes to Le Morne in the southwest; and the Grand Port Range in the southeast, stretching 24km (15 miles) from Mount Lagrave to the mouth of Grande Rivière Sud-Est (Southeast). Also in the south are the smaller Savanne Mountains, just above Souillac.

(The names of operators are given in brackets – see Directory for details.)

Moka Range
Pieter Both (820m/2,690ft)
With a precariously balanced head-shaped boulder on top, this is the highest mountain in north Mauritius and one of the most difficult to climb, taking seven to nine hours. It's worth it, though, for the stunning 360-degree views. Suitable for ages 16 years and upwards (Chazal, Otélair Ltée, Vertical World).
Le Pouce (812m/2,664ft)
See p44 (Vertical World).

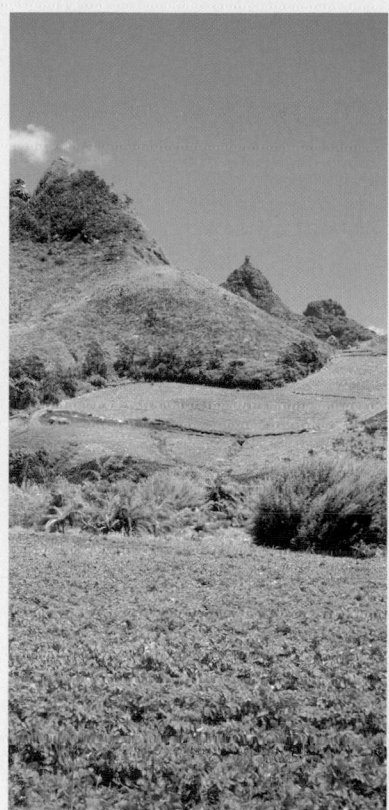

Pieter Both in the Moka Mountains

Black River Chain
Black River Peak (828m/2,717ft)
You may also see this signposted as Piton de la Petite Rivière. See p63 (Yemaya Adventures and others).

Corps du Garde (780m/2,560ft)
For fairly fit hikers, a climb up this mountain that looms over the town of Quatre Bornes affords a view over Mauritius' main inland cities and the west of the island (Yanature).

Montagne du Rempart (545m/1,788ft)
On the west coast behind Casela Nature and Leisure Park, the dramatically shaped Montague du Rempart. Mark Twain, who visited the island in 1896, referred to this mountain as the 'Pocket Matterhorn'. The final stretch is a steep rock climb. The climb and descent will take around five hours.

Le Morne Brabant (555m/1,821ft)
Le Morne Brabant must be climbed with an expert guide, and has various levels of difficulty. It takes four hours and there is an optional Tyrolean traverse across a crevasse on a 25m (82ft) zipline over a 450m (1,476ft) drop! (Yanature, Chazal)

Trois Mamelles (629m/2,064ft)
This imaginatively named ('Three Breasts') mountain lies in the foothills.

Grand Port Range
Lion Mountain (480m/1,575ft)
This may seem an easy half-day climb, but it becomes technical in parts and the slopes are slippery when wet. The trail leads right up the lion's 'back' to its 'head' for great views over the southeast (Otélair Ltée).

Savanne Mountains
Piton Savanne (704m/2,310ft)
With beautiful views over the south coast, there is a chance to see the pink pigeon (Vertical World).

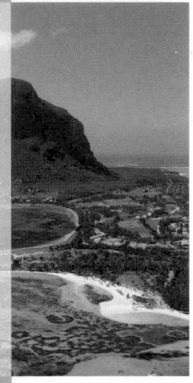

Drive: Curepipe to Gris Gris

This full-day drive passes through some of the most varied and exciting scenery on the island, from the plains to the highest peak in the densely forested interior and along the wild southwest coast. (See pp153–6 to choose a restaurant with a view.)

The drive covers 73km (45 miles) and will take around 8 hours.

Passing the Curepipe Gardens, turn left following the sign to Grand Bassin, and left again at La Marie and head up to Plaine Champagne. After about 7km (4 miles), opposite the Petrin Information Centre turn left along the road signposted to Grand Bassin. A 33m (108ft)-tall statue of Shiva signals the car park.

Map legend:
- ○ Large Town
- ○ Small Town
- ★ Start of Drive
- Motorway
- Main Road
- Minor Road
- POI

Map labels: Floréal, Curepipe, Domaine des Aubineaux, Baie du Tamarin, Tamarin, Henrietta, B70, Midlands, A3, Tamarin Mt 548, Tamarin Falls Reservoir, Mare aux Vacoas, M2, Nouvelle France, Grande Rivière Noire, Black River Visitors' Centre, Mt Brise Fer 622, Black River, Black River Gorges National Park, Petrin Information Centre, Pont Colville, N, Petite Rivière Noire, Black River Peak 828, Grand Bassin, Grand Bois, Case Noyale, Chamarel, Plaine Champagne, Bois Chéri Tea Factory, B88, Île aux Bénitiers, Chamarel Coloured Earth, Mt Cocotte 771, Pitoh Savanne 704, Rivière Dragon, Le Morne Brabant 555, B9, Chamarel Falls, Bassin Blanc, A9, L'Embrasure, Flinders Memorial, Baie du Cap, Chemin Grenier, Rivière des Anguilles, Baie du Cap, St Martin, Beau Champ, B89, St Aubin, Bel Ombre, B9, Îlot Sancho, Surinam, La Roche qui Pleure, Souillac, Gris Gris

Scale: 0 — 4km / 0 — 2 miles

1 Grand Bassin

An hour's walk on the circular path around this crater lake and Hindu pilgrimage site includes the Hanuman temple atop the hill.

Return to the car park and retrace your route, and then turn left opposite the Petrin Information Centre. Turn right at the next small roundabout. After about 5km (3 miles), stop at the car park with signs to Black River Peak.

2 Black River Peak viewpoint

Looking down the impressive Black River Gorges to the mountains beyond, to the left is the Black River Peak, at 828m (2,717ft) the highest point in Mauritius, with a lovely waterfall opposite.

Continue across Plaine Champagne and, coming out of the trees, wind down to Chamarel. Turn left to visit the Chamarel Coloured Earth, or continue straight on, turning left on to the B9 at Case Noyale. After 4km (2½ miles), the bare rock face of Le Morne Brabant will loom to the right, and about 10km (6 miles) later, you'll arrive at Baie du Cap.

3 Baie du Cap inlet

Perhaps the most stunning stretch of road on the island, the road winds beside the wild coast and by pretty untouched coves, into this steep inlet with rock overhangs and caves in the lush foliage.

Just past the huge rock at the end of the bay that marks an ancient boundary, make a stop at the Flinders Memorial, on the right by the sea.

4 Flinders Memorial

This bronze monument marks the unplanned six-year stay of the famous explorer Matthew Flinders. Arriving at Baie du Cap, he was arrested by the French as a spy (*see box on p64*).

Continue along the B9 for about another 10km (6 miles), and look out for a rocky island on your right, close to the shore.

5 Îlot Sancho

The first island taken by the British in 1810, before the historic battle of Grand Port. For a little adventure, wade out to this rocky outcrop and take the path under the trees to an anchor thought to be from a pirate ship.

Continue another 7.5km (4½ miles). Turn right at the sign to the Social Security Office which brings you opposite the Robert Edward Hart Memorial Museum.

6 Robert Edward Hart Memorial Museum, Souillac

Mauritius' most famous poet lived and wrote in his home here in the 1940s and 1950s. It's now a museum dedicated to his work.

Facing the museum, turn left to arrive at Gris Gris car park.

7 Gris Gris

A cliff-top viewpoint over a wild sea that pounds on to basalt rocks by a beach below, Gris Gris is the place to taste the wild south coast.

Return to Souillac and join the A9 for a speedier return to Curepipe.

Pirates and treasure

Although Madagascar and Réunion were most popular with Indian Ocean pirates in the 17th century, Mauritius was also a haven. Close to shipping routes, but far enough away to discourage pursuit, with a rugged shoreline ideal for hiding after an attack, and bays and creeks to stash treasure, hopeful hunters dig even today.

Pirate sites along the coast of Mauritius were left untouched for more than 200 years, but as some pirates died in fights or were shipwrecked, bounty hunters came to dig in hope of finding abandoned treasure during the 1900s. Some got lucky. Menon Prayag, a sugar baron from Rivière du Rempart district, inherited his wealth from his great-grandfather who accidentally stumbled upon treasure while working as a poor immigrant labourer. Just a few years ago, a fisherman came across two carved heads stuck in the coral near Baie du Tombeau. These carvings were originally being taken back to Europe on the shipwrecked *Banda*, and were probably washed into view by a cyclone. Fishermen here also claim to have seen the ghost of La Buse (*see opposite*) sitting on the rocks with his sword across his knees, shouting to them that his treasure was buried nearby. One of the Dutch commanders of Mauritius, Captain Hubert Hugo, was once a pirate, and, even after the departure of the Dutch in 1710, Mauritius remained a favourite pirate

The pirate influence is everywhere, even in this casino in Port Louis

A 'pirate' ship at Île aux Cerfs

spot until the French settlers came in 1721 and ended the golden age of pirateering.

La Buse (the Buzzard)

La Buse was one of Mauritius' best-known pirates. Born Captain Olivier Le Vasseur in Calais, France, in the 17th century, he arrived in Mauritius around 1720, en route capturing a Portuguese ship, the *Vierge-du-Cap*, in Bourbon (present-day Réunion). La Buse continued to plunder ships in the area until 1730 when he was captured. On the day of his hanging, La Buse is said to have thrown a piece of parchment to the crowd, shouting, 'Find my treasure he who can!' On the parchment was a cryptogram showing the site, starting a treasure hunt that stretched from the Seychelles through Mauritius and Réunion, to the southern tip of Madagascar. In Mauritius, treasure hunters dug at Klondyke (Black River) in 1902 and 1912, Walhalla (Black River) in 1925, Pointe Vacoas (La Cambuse) in 1926, and Saint Antoine

(Belmont at Poudre D'Or) in 1933. Is the treasure still there? Nobody knows.

Buried treasure

There may or may not be any treasure left in Mauritius, but there is no doubt that it was buried here, as signs designed to help pirates return to the right spot can still be seen today. As well as documents, maps, plans and cryptograms, the pirates carved signs such as a tortoise, pirate's boot, bull's eyes, arrows, crosses and other inscriptions in rock. Unfortunately, many historic sites are being destroyed by the mechanical diggers of treasure hunters, and Mauritius' history is in danger of being lost. There are currently no organised pirate tours on the island, but look out for pirate signs if you're visiting the following places, mostly in the south: Poudre d'Or village, Pointe du Diable (Devil's Point), the National History Museum in Mahébourg, Île des Deux Cocos, Souillac and Îlot Sancho. *Pirate Secrets of Mauritius* is available in bookshops on the island.

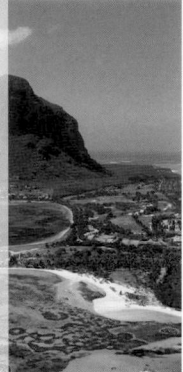

The east

With many of the island's best hotels and a coastline blessed with pretty coves and long sandy beaches, the east coast is associated with glitz and glamour. It's also a mecca for all manner of watersports. Cooled by the sea breeze, which makes it good for windsurfing and kite-surfing, this coast has the country's favourite island playground – Chazal. Inland, it boasts the island's largest open-air market in the village of Flacq.

PORT LOUIS

Domaine Les Pailles

Bon Accueil

A2

Le Waterpark

Belle Mare Plage

B49

Centre de Flacq

B59

Eureka

Union Flacq

M2

A7

Quartier Militaire

Rivière Sèche Bel Air

Île de l'Est

Quatre Bornes

Île aux Cerfs

B2

Phoenix

Montagne Blanche

B27

Grand Rivière Sud Est

Floréal

Curepipe

L'Étoile

Kawal Nagar

Domaine des Aubineaux

Mt Lagrave
638

Domaine L'Étoile

Henrietta

Midlands

Eau Bleue Reservoir

Anse Jonchée

Banane

Lion Mt
480

The Kestrel Valley

Domaine de Lagrave

Le Val Nature Park

Vieux Grand Port

Black River Gorges National Park

Domaine des 7 Vallées

Grand Bassin

A10

River Chaux

Mahébourg

Île aux Aigrettes

Bois Chéri Tea Factory

Grand Bois

M2

Piton Savanne
704

A9

Sir Seewoosagur Ramgoolam

Blue Bay

Bassin Blanc

B8

Île des Deux Cocos

Chazal

St Aubin

Rivière des Anguilles

Senneville

Souillac

Gris Gris

La Roche qui Pleure

N

○ ....Large Town
○ ....Small Town
■ ....POI
▭▭▭ ....Motorway
▬▬▬ ....Main Road
——— ....Minor Road
✈ ....Airport

0   5km
0   3 miles

Belle Mare Plage/Beach

Stretching from Trou d'Eau Douce to Pointe de Flacq, Belle Mare is regarded as one of the most beautiful beaches on the island, although motorised watersports can make it noisy. Off the beach is Solar Sea Walk (*departs from Grand Baie, see p39*) and the Pass, the east's most famous dive site.

There is little public transport to this beach, so take a taxi or hire car.

The museum at Bois Chéri Tea Factory

Bois Chéri Tea Factory

The modern Bois Chéri Tea Factory and museum offer a self-guided informative exhibition followed by an interesting and informative tour of the tea factory (or film in winter). Then, a short drive beside the tea fields leads to a DIY tea tasting or lunch at a former basic hunting lodge with a panoramic view of the south.

Bois Chéri Tea Estate, Grand Bois. Tel: 617 9109. Open: Mon–Fri 8.30am–4pm, Sat 8.30am–1.30pm, Sun 9am–4pm (Mon–Fri arrive before noon to see the factory process, Sat before 10am, Sun no process); in winter, the factory opens Wed am only. Drive, take a taxi or go on the Tea Route excursion.

Domaine des Aubineaux

Reached through a tunnel of bamboo, Domaine des Aubineaux is a whitewashed house with blue shutters overlooking a manicured garden built in 1872. It only opened to the public in 2000, when the last member of the family died. Everything has been left as it was – gorgeous wooden furniture imported from all over the world in teak and oak, and with items such as a marble stand-alone bathtub. Interesting side rooms reveal paintings of colonial houses now knocked down by cyclones. Tea and crêpes with jam are served in the café across from the house.

Curepipe. Tel: 676 3089. www.laroute duthe.mu. Open: daily 9am–5pm. Admission charge; cheaper if booked as part of the Tea Route. By hire car or taxi or on the Tea Route excursion.

Domaine L'Étoile

The pretty thatched eco-chalets nestling in a valley backed by mountains and fronted by sugar-cane fields were originally built as a film set for *Paul & Virginie* (1972), based on the island's most popular legend (*see p15*). They are now Domaine L'Étoile's reception and restaurant, where an authentic

Mauritian buffet lunch is served after activities. Both L'Étoile and Ferney, a neighbouring estate, also offer ecotourism on 15,200ha (38,000 acres) of land. Three-hour quad-biking trips visit deer-filled forested mountains with ebony trees and cinnamon, past coffee and vanilla plantations to full-day circuits to Falaise Rouge, a house with a view over the historic southeast. Five treks are offered, including an easy, botanical one, as well as mountain-biking circuits and horse riding. The archery course, using traditional bows with 20 targets in a 10ha (25-acre) forest clearing, is unique to Mauritius.

L'Étoile and Ferney, between Montagne Blanche and Kawal Nagar village. Tel: 433 1010 or 729 1050 (mobile). www.cieletnature.com (French only). Activities & lunch (included): daily 9.30am–1.30pm & noon–4pm. Book in advance. Admission charge. Note: in hunting season (Jun–Sept), activities are subject to change. Local bus to Mahébourg and then taxi or hire car to get there.

Domaine de Lagrave

Although not as beautiful as some, this small 202ha (500-acre) domaine is kept as close to its natural state as possible, and with no quad biking it is a good place to spot wildlife. Self-guided trekking is offered around Mount Lagrave, with trails divided into three levels of difficulty. The blue trail runs along the foothills for 3km (2 miles), the red trail up to the top for 6.5km (4 miles), and the black trail is a strenuous scramble up, rewarded with great views over Lion Mountain and the southeast coast. Fishing, archery, kayaking and rafting are also offered. A three-course table d'hôte lunch is served in very simple surroundings on request.

Village Banane, Eau Bleu. Open: daily 9am–4pm. Book in advance. Admission charge.

The thatched roofs of Domaine L'Étoile

A Ylang Ylang tree in the Kestrel Valley

Domaine des 7 Vallées

The owner of this estate was the pioneer of eco-adventure parks. It is now a wilderness of more than 4,000ha (almost 10,000 acres) and lies in the centre of the island, near Curepipe. Activities on land include quad biking with a stop at a waterfall and a mountain bike and trekking circuit. Sea ventures include regular fishing trips, island-hopping and pirogue regattas. An adventurous game menu – deer and wild boar – is cooked over a wood fire and served in the hunting lodge, along with rum produced to an ancestral recipe.

Ligne Barrique, Mare aux Vacoas. Tel: 631 3336. www.domainedes7vallees. com. Open: daily 9am–5pm.

Île aux Cerfs

Named after the stags (*cerfs*) that once lived here, this island paradise surrounded by a sand bar just off the east coast is the place to flop or loll in the shallows. Stalls selling *pareos* (sarongs) and surfwear vie with the banana-boat-ride sellers, but you can still find a calm spot on the sand, away from the boat jetty. This island, among the top sites in Mauritius, is not as small as it looks; measuring around 300ha (741 acres), it takes a couple of hours to walk around it. At low tide, it's possible to wade across to Île de L'Est, but be aware of the currents and motorboats in this narrow causeway. There are two restaurants on the island, of which **Paul and Virginie** is the best for an elegant fish lunch (*open: daily noon–3pm*). The speciality at the rustic

(*Cont. on p82*)

DUTCH REMAINS

Vlak means 'flat ground' in Dutch, and Flacq is the only town on the east coast. It was covered in ebony forest back in the dodo's time. It's now known for its large, lively market.

The Tea Route

It takes two days to process tea, three months to mature it and three minutes to drink it ...

Next to water, tea is the second-most common beverage consumed worldwide. A priest first brought tea plants from China to Mauritius, but it wasn't until the 1960s that plantations appeared. Now 40sq km (15sq miles) is under cultivation, mainly in the cooler, wetter, central part of the island. Mauritius has three tea producers: La Flora, Corson and Bois Chéri. The Bois Chéri Tea Factory produces 7,000 tonnes a year alone, and the crop is now second to sugar cane.

The tea plant is a dense bush with deep roots that can withstand cyclones. The tea pickers' art, plucking the top two to three young leaves and throwing them into a basket on their backs, is done mainly by women who start work around 4am. The leaves are then transported to the factory where they are dried, chopped, fermented, cleaned and sifted in preparation for storing, sorting, blending and packing.

La Route du Thé (the Tea Route) is an excursion offered by the Bois Chéri

Signs will direct you to tea tastings

Tea Estate, which has produced tea for over 100 years. As the organised tour includes a tasting and lunch, it's the best way to do it.

The four- to five-hour route kicks off at Domaine des Aubineaux in Curepipe, the elegant colonial home of the estate's owner which was built in 1872. The house has been left as it was when the family lived here, with furniture from all over the world and an extensive display of photographs. The road then winds across Plaine Champagne for 15km (9 miles) before dipping into the cheery Bois Chéri Tea Factory and museum, which has a self-guided informative exhibition on tea and the old machinery, and an interesting tour around the factory before a tea tasting at a former hunting lodge. Black Label is top-quality tea, and Paul & Virginie is the strongest. This is DIY tea bags with baby scones (on request) – but worth it for the panoramic view of the south. For a novelty gift, pick up a

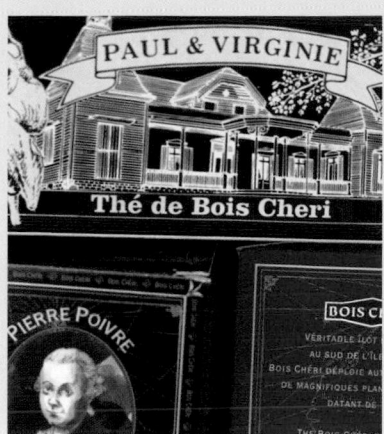

Tea from the Bois Chéri estate

packet of coconut-flavoured Le Dodo tea, made by the Bois Chéri Tea Company. Other flavours include vanilla, lemon and passion fruit.

A traditional Mauritian set lunch is served at the elegant Le Saint Aubin, 12km (7½ miles) south and five minutes' drive from the pounding sea at Gris Gris. A sugar plantation house set in tropical gardens, owned by the same family, it was built in 1819. If tea has led to a taste for something stronger, like a Vaco cocktail with vanilla rum and coconut, there's a guided tour around the tiny rum distillery here – the only place on the island to produce agricultural rum – and a chance to learn about vanilla production.

To book, tel: 626 1513/1730. Factory: Open: daily (summer); Wed am (winter). www.larouteduthe.mu

VANILLA AS VIAGRA

Vanilla is a member of the orchid family, and of 100 types only three are cultivated. Vanilla Bourbon is cultivated in Mauritius and takes nine months to reach maturity. It's a popular flavouring here – found in everything from tea and cocktails to desserts. Vanilla is also a natural aphrodisiac, which is why it's also used for candles and mood-setting scents.

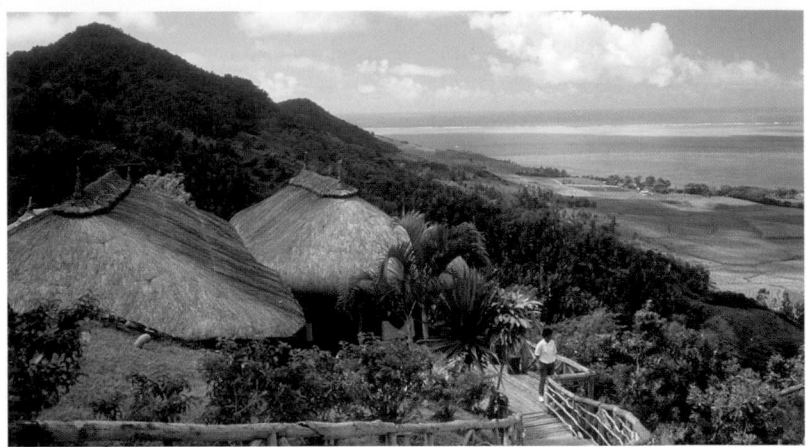

The stunning view from the Panoramour Restaurant in the Kestrel Valley

Sands Bar, a great place to hang out in rattan armchairs in the afternoon, is Planter's Punch (*open: daily 9.30am–5pm; snacks served 11.30am–4.30pm*). For the active, there's every watersport imaginable here, including parasailing, speedboats and a new undersea walk. For golfers, a game in one of the world's most beautiful settings can be booked through **Le Touessrok Hotel** (*Trou d'Eau Douce; tel: 402 7400; www.letouessrokresort.com*) across the water. *Half-hourly ferry: 8am–5pm (last boat back) from the public beach at Trou d'Eau Douce. Weekends, when it tends to get crowded, are best avoided. No admission charge – boat fare only.*

The Kestrel Valley

The Kestrel Valley was the first sugar estate to be turned into an eco-park, although now only a quarter of its original size at 400ha (1,000 acres). It's a tranquil place for 40-minute to 2-hour walks through lush vegetation, ancient trees and panoramic views. It's also the best place to encounter the Mauritius kestrel, the island's only bird of prey, as well as Java deer, wild boar and tropical birds. The alfresco Panoramour Restaurant has one of the island's best lunchtime views – of the Bambous Mountains sloping into an aquamarine sea. It also serves perhaps the most adventurous menu, with items such as roasted wild boar and deer curry. Included in the property is a Ylang Ylang Essences Garden, which has a tiny

THE FLOWER OF FLOWERS

Ylang Ylang was originally brought to Mauritius from the Philippines by Pierre Poivre in 1750, and planted in Pamplemousses (*see p42*). A long, yellow flower with a delicate scent, called 'the flower of flowers' by perfumers and mainly used as a fixer for an aromatherapy oil, it's useful against stress, anxiety and insomnia, high blood pressure and tiredness.

distillery where guests can discover how the essential oil is made. Five essential oils – Ylang Ylang, Lemongrass, Eucalyptus, Camphor and Pink Pepper – can be bought in the shop.

Although it can be viewed year-round, the most interesting time to go is between October and April when the Ylang Ylang tree flowers, and the distillery is working. If you want to stay, seven romantic, African-style eco-chalets are tucked away on the property. *Anse Jonchée. Well signposted, it's about 3km (2 miles) up a private road just past Vieux Grand Port. Tel: 634 5097. www.kestrelvalley.com. Open: daily 9am–4pm. Admission charge. Go by hire car or taxi.*

Le Saint Aubin

This is the family home of Pierre de St Aubin who started a sugar factory in 1819, and the estate surrounding this elegant mansion now produces rum and grows vanilla and anthurium flowers. The table d'hôte Creole lunch in the elegant dining room is the highlight, but a stroll around the house reveals authentic furnishings and photographs of colonial times.

'Maison du Rhum' is one of the few places on the island to produce agricultural rum: that is, from the first pressing of the sugar cane. See the juice crushed out of the sugar cane and all the stages of production before a tasting in the bar and an optional pre-lunch rum cocktail on the veranda. Across the gardens, scattered with wooden benches under the trees, is the Vanilla House with a small film on vanilla production, museum and greenhouse with both vanilla and anthurium flowers. *Rivière des Anguilles. Tel: 626 1513. Email: lesaintaubin@intnet.mu. www.larouteduthe.mu. Open: daily 9am–5pm. Admission charge; cheaper booked as part of the Tea Route excursion. By hire car or taxi or as part of the Tea Route excursion.*

Le Waterpark

This waterpark, with giant slides, wave pool and crazy river ride, is one of the few family attractions on the east coast and great for young children. There is a restaurant, kiosk and shop on site; bring flip flops as it can get hot underfoot. *Coastal Road, Belle Mare. Tel: 415 2626. www.lewaterpark.intnet.mu. Open: daily 10am–4pm. Admission charge.*

Vanilla is grown on the Le Saint Aubin estate

THE SOUTHEAST

All visitors to Mauritius arrive in the southeast, as this is where the airport is situated. However, the area is surprisingly untouristy and, unless staying around here, few visitors return. Romantic ruins, monuments, sites of historic battles and museums make the southeast a fascinating trip through Mauritius' colonial history. This part of the island has a feel of the old Mauritius in the villages and unspoilt coastal scenery, and it remains untouched by mass tourism. It is home to ecotourism parks and reserves, the largest animal park and a wilder, less visited coast, as well as several great new restaurants. The southeast also hosts Mauritius' only Marine Park, Blue Bay, one of the top spots for snorkelling, and the only offshore nature reserve, Île aux Aigrettes, thought to have been the last home of the mysterious dodo.

Blue Bay

The closest public beach to Mahébourg, Blue Bay has the most stunning underwater scenery close to shore on the island. The Blue Bay Marine Park is a protected area and, for that reason, visitors are encouraged to go on glass-bottom boat trips, or organised snorkelling excursions to preserve it. But if you can, launch yourself from the coastguard's office and snorkel over some breathtaking coral.
Glass-bottom boat trips travel over the Marine Park from the jetty. Call first to avoid rogue operators. Recommended

EXCURSIONS FROM BLUE BAY

Several operators organise excursions from Blue Bay, mostly starting from Pointe Jerome near the Preskil Hotel. Tam Tam Travel & Tours offers day trips with Preskil's catamaran to Île aux Cerfs up the coast, as well as two-hour boat trips out to Île aux Aigrettes. Joceyln and his daughter at Totof provide off-the-beaten-track small-group day trips on a purpose-built trimaran to the islands off the southeast coast – Île de la Passe, Île aux Fous and Île Vacoas. This includes plenty of snorkelling opportunities and a barbecue lunch on one of the islands.
Totof. Tel: 751 1772. Email: boatotof@yahoo.com. Tam Tam Travel & Tours. Tel: 631 8642. Email: tamtnt@intnet.mu. Call in advance to book. Excursion fee.

operators include Totof and Tam Tam Travel & Tours. See box above.

Gris Gris

Excursions on this coast always include a stop at Gris Gris, a dramatic cliff top overlooking a rough sea that gives a taste of the wilder side of Mauritius. The waves pound basalt rocks in front of a powder sand beach on this, the island's southernmost point. Steps lead down to the beach, and at very low tide it's possible to peek into caves under the cliff. Take a walk along the cliff top (*see pp88–9*) to really get away from it all.
Most people stop off on an excursion, but you can take public transport, taxi or hire car.

Île aux Aigrettes

A coral outcrop, surrounded by a limpid sea, about 1km (²/₃ mile) off the

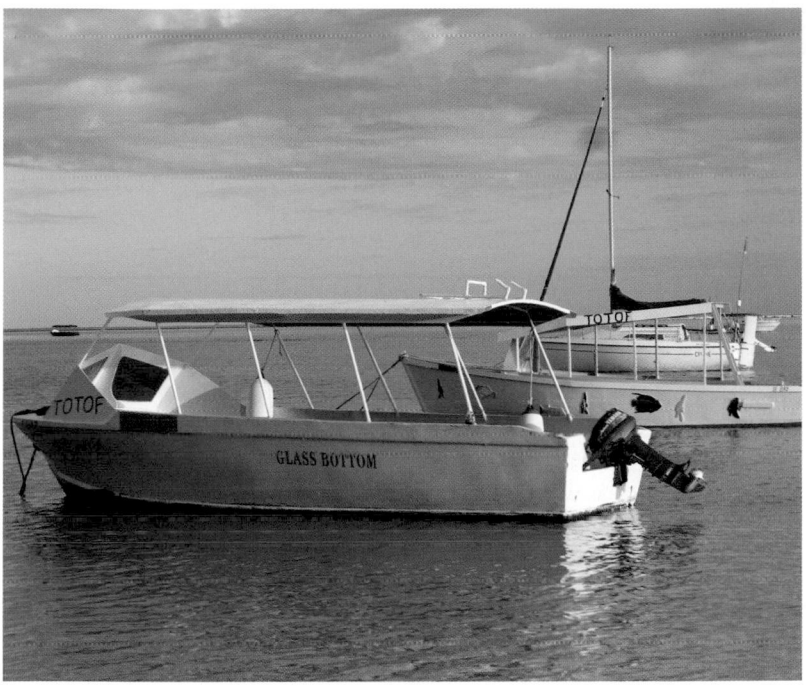

Glass-bottom boats at Blue Bay

coast of Mahébourg, Île aux Aigrettes (Egret Island) is the nearest visitors can get to the Mauritius of 400 years ago. This 25ha (62-acre) island, established as a nature reserve in 1985, may have been home to the last dodo, now remembered in bronze at the entrance, and has some of Mauritius' last remaining coastal forest with ebony, orchids and rare palms. Managed by the Mauritius Wildlife Foundation (MWF), it has become an international standard for the protection of natural resources and endangered species. Giant Aldabra tortoises lumber under the 7m (23ft)-high canopy, and endemic geckos and lizards live here. The trail here passes

20 endemic plants, with the rare Telfair skink in an enclosure. Île aux Aigrettes is a breeding ground for the pink pigeon, where it lives in the semi-wild.
Tel: 631 2396. www.mauritian-wildlife.org. Departures for guided tours
(Cont. on p90)

EXCURSION: KAYAKING UP THE GRANDE RIVIÈRE SUD-EST

At 34km (21 miles), Grande Rivière Sud-Est (Southeast), marking the boundary between Flacq and Grand Port districts, is the longest river in Mauritius. Catamarans or boats usually take visitors on it, but you could kayak the 20 minutes to a lovely waterfall with Carlie Ltée (*Tel: 263 0713. www.voyagesmaurice.net*).

Diving

Almost entirely surrounded by a barrier reef, with the overhangs and caves characteristic of a volcanic island, and clear warm waters and a good variety of marine life, Mauritius has some of the best dive sites in the Indian Ocean. From diving in aquarium-like areas filled with tropical fish and witnessing big fish such as tuna, wahoo and marlin, to diving in canyons or swimming with sharks, Mauritius provides something for both novice and advanced divers and, importantly, has friendly, professional and relaxed operators.

Fifty dive centres are registered with the **Mauritius Scuba Diving Association (MSDA)** (*Tel: 454 0011.*

Diving in Mauritius can be like swimming in a tropical aquarium!

www.msda.mu). Many are based in hotels, although there are some independent operators, mainly in Grand Baie. Diving is well regulated here, with most operators members of internationally recognised organisations such as the Professional Association of Diving Instructors (PADI), National Association of Underwater Instructors (NAUI) or Confédération Mondiale des Activités Subaquatiques (CMAS).

Three levels of diving are available on the island. Most centres offer beginner dives that lead to either an introductory certificate or an internationally accepted 1-star certificate. The second level is for qualified divers with an updated logbook who can join one of two dive times (*9.30am & 1.30pm*) operated by most of the dive centres, six days a week. Most of these dives are to a depth of 10–30m (33–98ft). The third level, for experienced divers only, is deep diving, down to 60m (197ft), as well as diving in less frequented areas. Specialised divers often head for the virgin sites in nearby Rodrigues (*see p107*). Take a recent medical certificate, and some operators may also want to see divers' logbooks. As experienced divers will know, make sure you allow 24 hours between diving and taking a flight.

Diving here is year-round, although the best time is from October to December and March to April. Diving is also regional, with the greatest concentration and widest range of dive sites in the north, including rewarding diving around the northern offshore islands. Dive centres tend to cover the dives in their own regions.

The most popular dive sites lie off the west coast, around Flic en Flac and Trou aux Biches. Wreck-diving adds a mystique and historic element to diving here.

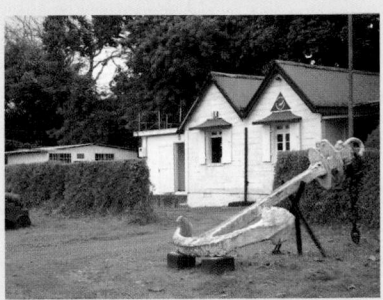

Mauritius Underwater Group's clubhouse at Phoenix

TOP FAVOURITE SITES

Aquarium, Trou aux Biches: As its name suggests, this is a place to see a wide variety of corals and fish, some quite rare. It's a good site for beginners.

Cathedral, Flic en Flac: The island's top dive, this is a huge cave full of colourful tropical fish, and drops off to around 30m (100ft) at its deepest point.

Passe St Jacques, Le Morne: Sightings of black-tip sharks are guaranteed on this drift dive.

Water Lily, Trou aux Biches: This is a well-established site featuring three water barges sunk in 1980.

Whale Rock, Grand Baie: This is a suitable drift dive around submerged black slabs of rock. At its deepest point, it includes canyons and caves.

DIVE CENTRES
North
Atlantis Diving School
Trou aux Biches. Tel: 265 7172.
West
Exploration Submarine
Flic en Flac. Tel: 453 8450.

MSDA
To find a dive centre near your resort, *tel: 454 0011. www.msda.mu*

Qualified divers can chat to resident divers at Mauritius Underwater Group's (MUG's) Tuesday-night BYO BBQ at its clubhouse in Phoenix. The only member of the British Subaqua Club in the southern Indian Ocean, MUG founded diving in Mauritius and also rents out equipment.

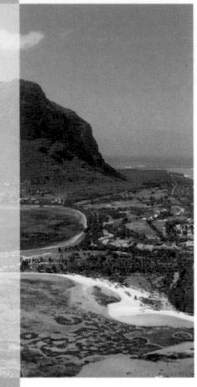

Drive: From Gris Gris to Blue Bay

The wild south coast is the least explored region of Mauritius. This drive incorporates short walks from the best viewpoints with unusual rock phenomena, and can be extended to a full day, with an excursion to La Vanille Réserve des Mascareignes.

The drive covers a distance of 45km (28 miles) and will take between 4 and 6 hours.

Starting from Souillac, take the road signed to Gris Gris or 'witch', and park above the cliffs.

1 Gris Gris viewpoint

Where a wild sea crashes over basalt rocks, from here there are great views along the coast. This is one of the most popular viewpoints on the island.

Take the steps down to the beach and at the bottom turn left down a small, rough grassy track. A short climb up a bank brings you into a clear track on the top of the cliff among the filao *trees. After 15 minutes, at the end of the beach is a flat grassy area on a promontory.*

2 La Roche qui Pleure

The name La Roche qui Pleure (The Rock that Weeps) refers to the lower rocky outcrop below the promontory, often awash with water. The rock shaped like a hat in the sea, to the right, is said to be the Gris Gris or 'witch'.

The path left up the hill takes you further, coming to an abrupt and dramatic end after 15 minutes, where a river cuts through to the sea. Retrace your steps to the car park. Drive on the A9 out of Souillac towards Rivière des Anguilles. Turn right on the B8 towards the airport. To visit La Vanille Réserve des Mascareignes, follow the signposts on the one-way system around the village until you reach the entrance.

3 La Vanille Réserve des Mascareignes

A crocodile and tortoise breeding project, there's at least a couple of hours' worth here for children and adults. There's also the Hungry Crocodile restaurant, a good lunch stop.

Continue along the B8. At L'Escalier, turn right at the police station, past the Savanna Sugar Estate mill. After about 4km (2½ miles) is the end of the road and Le Souffleur.

4 Le Souffleur

Look over the railings towards the rock in the sea where, infrequently, spray spurts out of a hole at high tide. It once roared 18m (60ft) up through this natural blowhole.

Walk east, or left if facing the sea, along the path from Le Souffleur. Follow the rocky road and flattened grassy path alongside the cliffs for about 30 minutes, or 2km (1¼ miles), to reach Pont Naturel.

5 Pont Naturel (Natural Bridge)

Least known and visited of the tourist sights, rocks have formed a natural bridge over the sea here. You can walk over it, at your own risk.

Retrace your steps and then drive back towards L'Escalier and turn right. Follow the B8 to Plaine Magnien. Join the motorway near the airport and turn left. At the next roundabout, turn right towards Mahébourg. After 4km (2½ miles), turn right towards Blue Bay.

6 Blue Bay

This public beach has the best underwater marine life close to shore on the island. Snorkel, take a glass-bottom boat or swim from the beach.

(1½ hours) are daily 9.30am, 10am, 10.30am, 1.30pm & 2pm. It's a 5-minute boat ride from Sun Jetty just below the Preskil Hotel, Blue Bay. Book tours in advance. Admission charge.

Robert Edward Hart Memorial Museum

Robert Edward Hart is Mauritius' most famous poet, awarded the Legion of Honour by France. Although he wrote in French, he was of British-Irish descent. If going down to Gris Gris, it's worth popping into this small museum in what was once his home, where his poems and personal objects are displayed.

Le Nef, Souillac. Follow the signs through the residential streets; it's close to Gris Gris. Tel: 625 6101. Open: Mon & Wed–Fri 9am–4pm, Sat 9am–noon.
Closed: Tue & Sun. Free admission.

La Vanille Réserve des Mascareignes

It was Charles Darwin who sent Aldabra tortoises here from the Seychelles to save them from extinction, and La Vanille, set up in 1985, is currently the only place in the world to breed them. They range in size from tiny hatchlings to Domino, who is now almost 100 years old. This is a

The creatures at La Vanille come in all shapes ...

... and sizes!

great place for young families as there is a jungle adventure playground and the chance to hold a baby crocodile (*Wed 11.30am; extra charge*). Around 500 tortoises live among the lush tropical foliage, although the main fascination may be with the thousands of Nile crocodiles (made into handbags and belts in the gift shop and served as fritters, kebabs and curry in the Hungry Crocodile restaurant). It takes 2 to 3 hours to look around this extended animal park with deer, cheeky Macaque monkeys, wild boar, iguanas, bats, an aquarium and even an insectarium, with one of the world's largest collections.

Senneville, 2km (1¼ miles) south of Rivière des Anguilles. Tel: 626 2503. www.lavanille-reserve.com. Open: daily 9.30am–5pm. Admission charge. Most people take an excursion here, but it's possible to get a bus to nearby, take a taxi or drive by hire car as it's well signed from various places.

WORD OF WARNING

Rochester Falls, 5km (3 miles) from Souillac, are the prettiest on the island, but it is unwise to visit them independently. Local residents have been known to demand money for jumping into the falls, and turn ugly when tourists refuse to pay. Some taxis refuse to go there.

HISTORIC SOUTHEAST

'The Lion Mountain dipping its toes in the bay of Mahébourg.'

Malcolm de Chazal, Mauritian poet

Mahébourg

Named after Mahé de Labourdonnais, 50 years after his death, Mahébourg was founded in 1804 by the French governor Charles Decaën, near the fort where the Dutch raised the first flag in 1598. It was once a busy port and a lively town with a racecourse during English rule. It is still characterful and, with fewer tourists than Port Louis, a place to taste the flavour of old Mauritius. If possible, visit on a Monday when the market brings the town to life. However, on any day, you can watch the action from the terraces of a few rustic restaurants on the main drag.

BERTRAND-FRANÇOIS MAHÉ DE LABOURDONNAIS

Born at Saint Malo in 1699, little did Bertrand imagine when he joined the Royal Navy as a ship boy at the age of ten that he would go on to be appointed governor of Île de France (present-day Mauritius) by the East India Company. Mahé de Labourdonnais, as he is known, took over in 1734, moving the capital from Mahébourg to the more sheltered Port Louis. As soon as he set foot on the island, he started on an 11-year development and construction programme that provided the colony with a road network and developed its agriculture. Bertrand was architect, engineer and constructor of Port Louis, and also waged a systematic war against the maroons (deserting slaves) and traded slaves from Mozambique.

Mahébourg has several claims to importance, being built on the bay of Grand Port, the first place the Dutch landed and the site of Mauritius' most famous battle. The city also has a pink-paved promenade, the Waterfront,

The National History Museum, Mahébourg

View across Grand Port Bay from Mahébourg

which makes a pleasant 1km (²/₃-mile) stroll, where you can pick up some *gajaks* (snacks) at one of the stalls and eat them looking out to sea. There's a monument to French and English seamen lost in the battle of Grand Port at Pointe des Régates (Regatta Point), a breezy headland that overlooks the bay where it took place and has views over Île aux Aigrettes and Île de la Passe, which defended the main route into Mahébourg Bay. Named after its sphinx-like shape, the 480m (1,575ft) Lion Mountain forms the moody

backdrop to the bay, and Dutch settlers are known to be buried at its foot.

National History Museum

Housed in an elegant 18th-century colonial house at the end of a driveway surrounded by woodland, the National History Museum is worth a visit just for the grand entrance, let alone Mahé de Labourdonnais' bed, and the bell from the shipwreck of *Le Saint-Géran* that inspired Mauritius' most famous legend (*see p15*). The ship was wrecked in 1744 carrying the first sugar refinery

Lion Mountain viewed through the mangroves at Dutch Monument

machinery from France to the island, but was only discovered in 1966. The museum always features in excursions to Mahébourg. It has rooms dedicated to the naval battle of 1810 and to the Dutch, French and British periods.
Tel: 631 9329. Open: Mon–Sat 9am–4pm, Sun 9am–noon. Free admission. Bus, taxi or hire car on the main route into Mahébourg.

Pointe du Diable (Devil's Point)

Odd compass readings experienced by ships passing this point are blamed on the devil that guards the treasure here. However, any possible pirate signs have long been removed as the French army moved here in the 1750s.

Rault Biscuit Factory

About 1km (²⁄₃ mile) north of Mahébourg, this family-run factory is on every tour of the southeast. A tour is more interesting than it sounds, as this family has been producing biscuits from manioc – a Creole root vegetable – by hand since 1870. It ends with a tasting of the biscuits imaginatively flavoured with custard, cinnamon, chocolate and coconut.
Signed from Cavendish Bridge, north of Mahébourg. Tel: 631 9559. Open: Mon–Fri 9am–3pm. Closed: weekends. Admission charge.

Fort Frederik Hendrik

Vieux Grand Port is the oldest settlement in Mauritius, now a fishing village with pirogues bobbing in the sea. Blink and you'd probably miss it. Few historical remains are left, apart from Fort Frederik Hendrik in a garden sloping to the sea, well signed at the northern end of the village. Here, visitors can walk through

THE BATTLE OF GRAND PORT

The battle of Grand Port raged from 20 to 28 August 1810, and is a source of pride for the French – it was the only battle they won in the Napoleonic Wars in the area, despite British trickery. The English and French captains, Willoughby and Duperré, both wounded, were nursed in what is now the National History Museum. Yet victory was short-lived. Having failed to take the island from the south, the British entered from Cap Malheureux at the island's most northerly tip, claiming the island as their own in December of the same year.

the 17th-century ruins of the first Dutch fortifications, with a French layer on top, for commanding views across the bay. The **Frederik Hendrik Museum** in the grounds houses well-planned exhibits of what was excavated here. In Bois des Amourettes (Young Lovers' Wood), in between here and the Ylang Ylang farm, French soldiers used to duel over girls they met here. Just off the coast are the caves of Salle d'Armes, where swords were also found, now only accessible by sea.

Frederik Hendrik Museum, Vieux Grand Port. This is an isolated part

LOOKING FOR LUNCH?

One of the few restaurants along this lonely coast, the rustic **Le Barachois** (*Anse Bambous, Vieux Grand Port. Tel: 634 5643. Open: daily 10am–6pm. Booking not necessary for lunch*), just before Devil's Point, specialises in lobster and crab farmed on the premises. It serves a great four-course lunch in a quiet spot beside the sea.

of the coast, easier to reach by hire car than bus. Tel: 634 4319. Open: Mon–Tue & Thur–Sat 9am–4pm, Sun 9am–noon. Closed: Wed. Admission charge.

The east

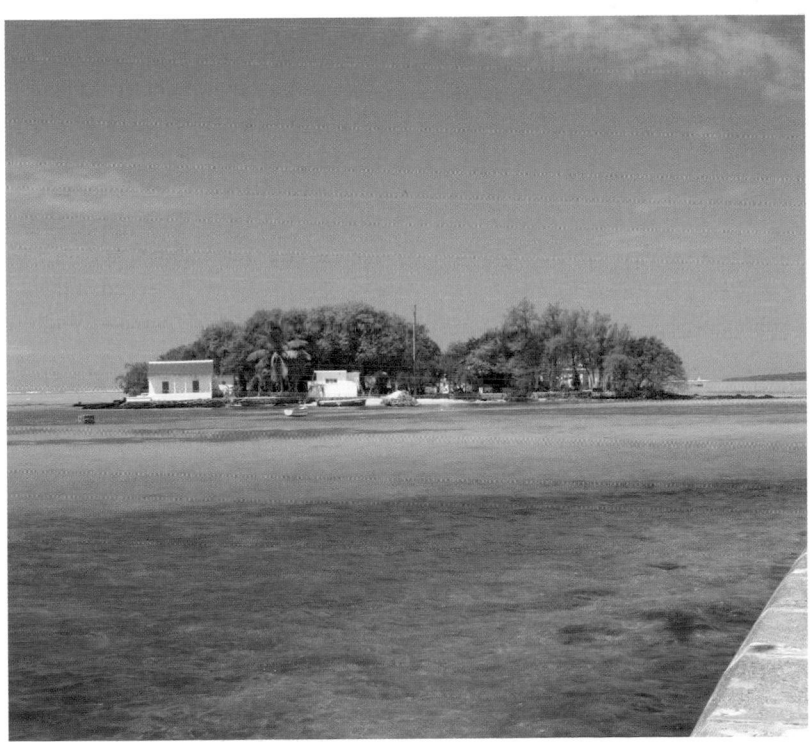

A private island in the bay of Grand Port

Eco-adventures on Mauritius

A wide choice of eco-adventures is
available on Mauritius, from climbing
the mountains, visiting pristine islands
off the coast, exploring an island
nature reserve, through hiking in the
national park to privately guided
excursions by kayak or bike. However,
the greening of Mauritius has been
led by the opening of ecotourism
playgrounds on vast private sugar
estates, with near-native forest
teeming with wildlife such as deer,
monkeys and rare birds.

NORTH

❶ Domaine Les Pailles, near Port Louis

The Domaine most suitable for
families, this 1,500ha (3,700-acre)

nature park at the foot of the
Moka Mountains offers guided horse
rides, tours by train and horse-drawn
carriage rides.
Les Guibies, Pailles.
Tel: 286 4225.
www.domainelespailles.net
(French only)

WEST

❷ Casela Yemen Nature Escapade, near Flic en Flac

Yemen has guided hiking, double-
quad, mountain biking, 4WD rides,
segway and buggies as well as an
African-style savanna where antelopes
and zebra roam (*see pp48–9*).
Cascavelle. Tel: 727 6076.
www.caselayemen.mu

EAST

❸ Domaine L'Étoile, near Montagne Blanche

Half-day quad, 4WD trips, botanical and other treks and mountain biking are offered through the forested mountains of this 15,380ha (38,000-acre) estate.
Tel: 433 1010 or 727 1050 (mobile).
www.cieletnature.com

SOUTHWEST

❹ Domaine Louisa, Chamarel

Parc Aventure is an army-style obstacle course through a forest, across bridges and up climbing nets, open to children aged six and upwards.
Tel: 234 5385/727 0869 (mobile).
www.parc-aventure-chamarel.com

❺ Chazal, east of Bel Ombre

The only zipline adventure park in the Indian Ocean, half-day courses run for 2km (1½ miles) over Rivière des Galets in Chamonix. River trekking is also available.
Tel: 622 7234 or 422 3117/3120 (mobiles).

❻ Frederica Nature Reserve, Domaine de Bel Ombre

The newest nature reserve to open, this offers half-day quad and 4WD adventures, trekking or day trip with trekking, and quads in a 1,012ha (2,500-acre) nature reserve with its own 150m (500ft) waterfall.
Tel: 623 5615/729 4498 (mobile).
www.domainedebelombre.mu

❼ Canyoning, Tamarin Falls

Abseil down a waterfall, canyon through waterpools and zipline as a grand finale. Stunning view from Tamarin Falls. Also available at five other locations (*see website*).
Tel: 697 5430, 254 6607 (mobile).
www.verticalworldltd.com

SOUTHEAST

❽ Domaine des 7 Vallées

Although it has moved premises, this domaine is still a favourite, offering quad biking to a waterfall as well as trekking, horse riding and mountain biking in over 4,000ha (9,884 acres) of wilderness (*see p79*).
Tel: 631 3336.
www.domainedes7vallees.com

❾ Beachcomber Sport & Nature

Beachcomber is currently the only hotel group to offer an ecotourism programme to its guests. Activities include mountain biking, kayaking and abseiling/canyoning.
Shandrani Hotel. Tel: 603 4343.
www.beachcomber-hotels.com.
Activities only available through Beachcomber hotels.

Drive: Phoenix to Devil's Point

This largely historic drive goes from the centre of the island through a pretty nature reserve to the major historic sites along the fascinating southeast coast. It's worth doing this drive on a Monday to catch Mahébourg's atmospheric weekly market.

The drive covers a distance of 43km (27 miles) and takes the best part of a day.

From Phoenix, take the motorway south past the Phoenix Brewery, taking a left at junction 16, signed 'Midlands', just past Curepipe. In Midlands village, turn right to Eau Bleue Reservoir and follow the road through Banane, until you see the signpost on the left to Le Val Nature Park, about 1km (⅔ mile) before Cluny. Take

the potholed track up through a gate (open: daily 6am–5pm) and down the hill. Tell the guardian you're going to Le Val.

1 Le Val Nature Park

Unless it's lunchtime, there's not much to keep you at Le Val. Just pay the small admission charge for this scenic drive that offers lovely views over Lion Mountain and the southeast coast as you descend to the park.

Continue through the reserve through St Hubert, and after 3km (2 miles) turn left past Riche en Eau sugar estate and drive through a pretty, quiet tree-lined road. Turn right at a roundabout towards the airport, and after 2km (1¼ miles) turn left to take the A10 to Mahébourg. Turn right if you want to take a side trip to Blue Bay. The National History Museum is on the left, as you enter Mahébourg.

2 National History Museum

The injured commanders of the French and English fleets were treated in this grand French colonial house surrounded by woodland, after the battle of Grand Port in 1810. Now, among the cannons and memorabilia lies the bell of the *Le Saint-Géran* that inspired Mauritius' most famous legend (*see p15*).

Continue into Mahébourg until you see the police station. Turn right after it, down Rue des Mariannes, and park at the Waterfront.

3 Mahébourg Waterfront

This paved promenade makes a pleasant 1km (⅔-mile) stroll. Surrounded by *gajak* (snack) stalls, it has monuments to soldiers and slaves, and views over the bay where the famous battle of Grand Port took place.

Continue driving through Mahébourg

until just over the River Chaux, with its stories of pirate treasure, and turn right to Vieux Grand Port (no sign).

4 Dutch Monument

This monument, to the right in the mangrove just below Lion Mountain, is where the Dutch first landed in 1598 and named the island Mauritius after the Dutch governor (*stadholder*) Prince Maurits Van Nassau.

Continue on the coast road past small fishing villages and Ferney Sugar Estate, and look out for the Fort Museum by the sea on your right after Vieux Grand Port.

5 Fort Frederik Hendrik

First built by the Dutch in 1638, a simple square wooden fort with cannons at each corner, the fort ruins now seen by the edge of the sea are French (*see pp94–5*). It had fallen into disrepair before the Battle of Grand Port in 1810.

Continue on, taking a left turn to visit the Ylang Ylang Essences Garden at The Kestrel Valley or straight on to Devil's Point.

6 Pointe du Diable (Devil's Point)

Built in the 1750s to protect Mahébourg Bay, the stonework defences here are among the finest 18th-century workmanship in Mauritius. The national monument on the hill gives lovely views over the bay (*see also p94*).

Excursions

Taking an organised excursion is the most popular and convenient way to see the sights around the island and couldn't be easier – just hop on a minibus, and go. A wide variety of organised excursions is on offer from all major hotels by a small number of well-regulated providers (*see opposite*). These range from half-day shopping trips, helicopter tours, and eco-adventures on a 4WD or quad bike, to undersea adventures or day trips by catamaran to pristine islands. Local providers, such as those who own glass-bottom boats at Blue Bay, also have their own excursions. In addition, a growing ecotourism offering includes privately guided tours, from forest walks and scaling mountains to getting active on a bike or kayak.

Land excursions

These include themed half- to one-day tours across regions, but not going too far afield, such as 'Island Souvenir', the 'Tea Route', the 'Sugar Adventure', and 'Journey into the Past', which visits Eureka. There are more elaborate themes such as 'Adventure in Paradise', usually visiting Domaine L'Étoile, or 'Nature and History', travelling from Mahébourg's National History Museum to the southeastern attractions of La Vanille Réserve des Mascareignes and out to Île aux Aigrettes. There are also regional tours focusing on attractions

Take a catamaran cruise to Tamarin Bay to see dolphins

in a region such as the 'Scenic South', with options to shop, or 'Casela Yemen Nature Escapade' in the west; plus Chamarel in 'Colourful South' and 'Exotic North', 'Adventurous Mauritius' and 'Beyond the Beaten Tracks' (Summertimes).

Sea excursions

Mainly by catamaran, these tend to be day-long excursions and include a barbecue lunch on board and time for snorkelling. They classically head east to the Grande Rivière Sud-Est and its waterfall before stopping at the island playground of Île aux Cerfs, west into Tamarin Bay to see the dolphins, or to the Northern Islands or on an underwater adventure. A popular full-day excursion also goes to Île aux Cerfs. Summertimes has a good selection. Some, such as Mautourco's, offer a sunset catamaran cruise. White Sand Tours allow guests to hire a catamaran or powerboat with skipper from Cap Malheureux to cruise the islands and see dolphins or have a barbecue on Île aux Bénitiers. Excursion operators also do the full range of undersea adventures.

Ecotourism excursions

These are privately guided, often tailor-made excursions, and tend to be geared towards active people, although many are suitable for families. Land excursions include

mountain biking in private reserves in the north and southwest, mountain climbing all around the island, and trekking, mainly in the Black River Gorges National Park, as well as the more extreme sports of canyoning and abseiling. Sea excursions include sea-kayaking around some of the lesser-known islands (*see pp96–7 and Directory for providers*).

Main excursion operators
Connections Tourism Management Ltd
Crater Lane, Floréal. Tel: 696 9933. Email: connect@intnet.mu
Mauritours
Rue S Venkatesananda, BP 125, Rose Hill. Tel: 467 9700. www.mauritours.net
Mautourco
84 Gustave Colin Street, Forest Side. Tel: 670 4301. www.mautourco.com
Summertimes
5 Avenue Bernardin de St Pierre, Quatre Bornes. Tel: 427 1111. www.summer-times.com
White Sand Tours
M1 Motorway, Cassis, Port Louis. Tel: 405 5200. www.whitesandtours.com

TAXI!

Looking for a reliable taxi for a personal excursion? Try Dave (*D&D Rapid Service. Tel: 750 0108*), who worked for an excursion company for 20 years. He is knowledgeable and speaks excellent English.

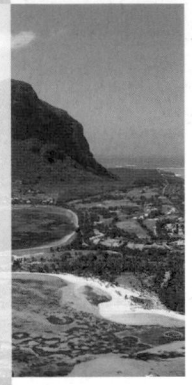

Getting away from it all

Although Mauritius is one of the most densely populated islands on earth, getting away from it all is easier than you might imagine. Inland in the southwest, the Black River Gorges National Park has a large swathe of forested hills criss-crossed with hiking trails, or why not climb a volcanic peak (see pp70–71) or visit a Domaine or ecotourism park (see pp96–7)? Out to sea, there are excursions to the paradise islands you've dreamed of (see below & p104) as well as Rodrigues Island, a 90-minute flight away.

ISLAND LIFE
North
Kayaking around Île d'Ambre (Amber Island)

Patrick Haberland's Yemaya Adventures, named after the African goddess of the sea, offers sea-kayaking expeditions around the little-visited Île d'Ambre (*see box opposite*). Expeditions are typically for a full day, and include optional snorkelling in the mangrove, a guided hike to the old ruins and a lunch stop at the nearby tiny island, Pointe Bernache. Modern double or single kayaks imported from South Africa are used, and the trips are tailor-made according to level and interest, and are all personally escorted. This activity is suitable for children of eight years and upwards.
*Yemaya Adventures based at Grand Gaube. Tel: 752 0046.
www.yemayaadventures.com. Adventures offered daily for a fee; lunch included. Book in advance.
Summertimes. Tel: 427 1111.
www.summer-times.com*

Southwest
Île aux Bénitiers (Clam Island)

Crescent-shaped Clam Island, known to the locals as 'Coco Island' because it's covered in coconut trees, lies in the lagoon off La Gaulette village near Le Morne and can be visited on a day trip by catamaran or kayak. Only 2km (1¼ miles) long and 0.5km (⅓ mile) wide, this tiny island has clear white beaches, without much sharp coral.

A Yemaya Adventures expedition around Île d'Ambre

Anemones and clownfish can be observed at Blue Bay

It's very private and not too deep, so ideal for swimming.

Croisières Évasion, Beau Bassin. Tel: 728 8109 (mobile). Depart: 9am, see dolphins at Tamarin and snorkel (30 mins), on island for 1½ hours, barbecue on board, back by 4pm.

Dolswim, Rivière Noire. Tel: 422 9281. www.dolswim.com. Depart: from Island Sports Hotel, Black River 8am, for a full day, swimming with dolphins in Tamarin plus a swim at Île aux Bénitiers. Summertimes (see opposite) offers a

similar itinerary on its 'Adrien's Dreams' cruise – a full-day luxury speed-boat trip. It's not recommended to take an ordinary boat from the beach.

AMBER ISLAND

Named after the ambergris once found there, Amber Island is important both ecologically and historically. Surrounded by mangrove, an important breeding ground for fish, it is also where the *Le Saint-Géran* was shipwrecked on 17 August 1744, giving birth to Mauritius' most famous book and legend, *Paul et Virginie* (see p15).

Southeast
Île des Deux Cocos
(Island of the Two Coconuts)

Visitors are met at the jetty here with cold, perfumed towels and sparkling wine. As you sink into luxurious white sofas in an open-sided tent next to a thatched bar serving tempting home-made rums, it's not difficult to believe in paradise. Offered exclusively by Naiade Resorts, this island excursion has all the luxury trappings that you'd expect, without the gimmicks. Small and not far from shore, with powder-white beaches, the island is idyllic and interesting – visitors can go on a glass-bottom boat or snorkel over the stunning reef of the Blue Bay Marine National Park nearby. Lunch is a highlight, with an excellent high-quality, plentiful buffet and faultless service.

A tour around the Folly here reveals a sumptuous Moroccan-style villa retreat with a bath, big enough for four, filled with rose petals. The Folly was built in 1925 by the British governor Sir Hesketh Bell to entertain his mistresses. Rumours of treasure led him to dig here and, suspiciously, he left for England soon after.

Bookings: Tel: 423 1752. Email: mariod@naiade.com or through Naiade hotels (www.naiade.com), which includes speedboat transport. Excursions daily from 10am until around 4pm. Excursion charge. Summertimes (Tel: 427 1111. www.summer-times.com) offers a full-day 'Islets Escapade' including Île aux Aigrettes.

ON LAND
North
Yemaya Adventures

Ex-cycling champion Patrick Haberland runs unique mountain-biking trips around this 12–25km (7$\frac{1}{2}$–15$\frac{1}{2}$ miles) of track, suitable for both beginners and advanced riders. The ride has a good variety of scenery, starting off along the coast before winding in between bush forest and joining the old railway line to visit some lava caves and then along shady trails into the exotic forest of Bras d'Eau. Patrick knowledgeably points out

Rodrigues Island is a short hop by plane from Mauritius

any wildlife en route – there's a chance of spotting the endemic and rare Paradise Flycatcher here – as well as endemic and indigenous plants. You also have a chance to explore the ruins of an old sugar mill. All adventures are personally led and can be tailor-made, but typically range from a gentle half day to longer and more challenging, depending on skill. Children aged 12 and over are welcome.

Yemaya Adventures, Grand Gaube. Tel: 752 0046. www.yemayaadventures.com. Excursions daily 9am–midnight; book in advance. Excursion charge. Clients need to get to the start point.

A deserted beach on Rodrigues Island

Rodrigues Island

Referred to as the anti-stress island, Rodrigues is a sleepy, rustic island with a laid-back charm. Here, women in straw hats spear octopus in the clear lagoon and fishermen still set sail in traditional wooden pirogues. Just 17.5km (11 miles) long and 8km (5 miles) wide, with a lagoon double its size, it's a place to go for relaxation and simplicity. With few cars in sight, Rodrigues offers Creole culture, large doses of fresh air, organic chicken and octopus, and around 20 secluded beaches.

Key places to visit include its capital, Port Mathurin, just seven streets wide; Trou d'Argent, 'The Money Hole', a wild cove where pirates once landed; Caverne Patate, where an hour's tour takes in stalagmites and stalactites; Île aux Cocos (Coconut Island), a white, sandy bird sanctuary where noddies

bob in the wind while visitors laze in the shallows; and the François Leguat Giant Tortoise and Cave Réserve.

Walking trails criss-cross the island, and it has a reputation as a good place for diving (there are three dive centres around the island; closed July and August), deep-sea fishing (marlin, skipjack tuna and sun fish; best October to April) and kite surfing (best May to September, based at the Mourouk Hotel). There is a Tyrolienne (zipline) in the centre of the island.

Air Mauritius offers flights to Rodrigues, four times a day in peak season. www.airmauritius.com. Demand is high, so book well ahead.

Pick up *A Guide to Rodrigues* and map from **Rodrigues Tourism Office** (*Tel: 832 0866*) and check out their useful website *www.tourism-rodrigues.mu*. A good range of adventure tours and activities is offered by **2000 Tours**, Port Mathurin. *Tel: 831 1894. Email: 2000trs@intnet.mu*

When to go

When planning activities, bear in mind that Mauritius has a microclimate, which means that it could be raining where you are with the sun shining a few kilometres away, or vice versa! Mauritius, like all places, has been experiencing 'untypical' weather of late due to climate change, so it is advisable to check on the weather before you go.

The island lies 20 degrees south of the equator, just above the tropic of Capricorn in the warm Indian Ocean, and has a tropical maritime climate. Although known primarily as a winter sun destination, with opposite seasons to Europe, Mauritius is generally sunny and pleasant on the coast throughout the year. The heat here rarely rises to uncomfortable levels, but sometimes it can get a little sticky and oppressive at night and some people find the northern coast in the height of summer unbearably hot. May to October, the island's winter, is warm and dry. Summer, from November to April, is hot, humid and rainy. During the height of the rainy season, from January to March, cyclones may strike the island, or pass nearby, meaning heavy rainfall and sometimes violent winds. The sea breeze blows steadily from the southeast all year round. July and August can see strong winds on the south and east coasts, which in summer transform into a welcome cooling breeze.

Average temperatures range from 17°C to 24°C (63–75°F) in August to between 23°C and 33°C (73–91°F) in January, and the water temperature is between 22°C and 27°C (72–81°F). The west and north are warmer and have less rain than the east and south. Average rainfall varies from around 900mm (35in) on the coast to

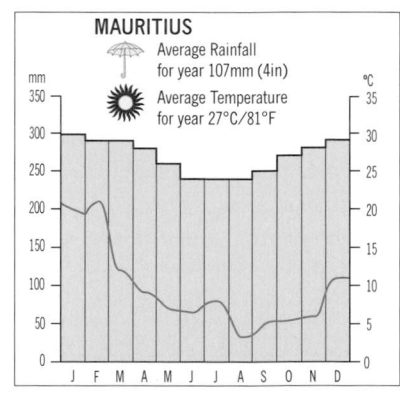

WEATHER CONVERSION CHART

25.4mm = 1 inch
°F = 1.8 × °C + 32

1,500mm (59in) inland. Curepipe has the highest rainfall of the inland towns, and it rains on Plaine Champagne at any time of year. Humidity is 75–85 per cent year-round.

December to January is peak season in Mauritius and best avoided. There's a big mark-up on holiday prices in December and also at Easter. Discounted holiday packages are more likely outside of French school holidays, and October and November are perhaps the best time to travel, when the price is right and the weather is good.

When to do what

November to April is the best time of year for diving, as waters are clear, calm and warm; June to July is the worst time. Divers and other watersports enthusiasts should avoid the peak cyclone season in January and February. June to August is best for surfing. The best deep-sea fishing (*see pp112–13*) is from October to April – the blue marlin season. Hikers, cyclists and climbers may prefer the cooler, drier months from June to September when there aren't as many mosquitoes at large. If you're into horse racing, the season runs from November to May, and if you want to catch one of the spectacular religious or cultural festivals, check the dates as these may vary from year to year (*see pp18–19*).

Sun and stormy skies near Le Val Nature Reserve

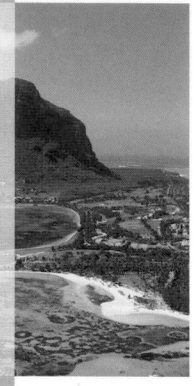

Getting around

Mauritius has one major highway, which snakes up the country from the airport in the southeast to the main tourist centre of Grand Baie in the north. Although the island is small, the generally narrow roads mean that driving anywhere takes time (although some roads will be widened in 2011). However, sightseeing is easy when all you need to do is board a minibus for a half- or full-day excursion, hire a car or taxi or, perhaps, travel by local bus for the experience.

Excursions

Most are reasonably priced and offer a selection of half- and full-day tours to all the main sites. With many of the large operators, the fee includes lunch and entrance (*see pp102–3 for details of operators and routes*).

Helicopter tours

Four-seater Bell Jet Ranger Helicopters, operated by Air Mauritius, offer sightseeing tours lasting from 15 minutes to an hour, giving a stunning bird's-eye view of the island. They also have 'heligolf' to the most beautiful golf courses, or 'helilunch', an hour's flight and drop-off for 2 hours for lunch somewhere special. Book through your tour operator, hotel, Summertimes (*see p102*) or directly (*Tel: 603 3754. Email: helicopter@airmauritius.com*).

Taxis

Tourist taxis are regulated and linked to hotels or provinces – this information is printed in a yellow panel on the driver's door. They're relatively inexpensive, with the cost of a journey varying depending on where you're staying and how long you're going to be. Hiring a taxi for a day is usually a convenient and cost-effective option. Tipping isn't expected, but is appreciated.

Public transport

A cheap and reasonably efficient bus service runs to every corner of the island, apart from the uninhabited parts of Plaine Champagne and Grand

TAXI TIPS

Although taxis have meters, fares can be negotiated for a return journey, and a cheaper rate is usually found away from the hotels. Taxis are used to taking tourists to the usual places, but not all drivers, even at hotels, speak English well. If you want to do anything unusual, buy a good map (*see p145*) to guide the drivers around. Also be aware that if you stop at the shops they suggest, most drivers are on commission.

Bassin. As the service is informal, you can be dropped off outside most of the tourist sites mentioned in this guide. Buses are particularly useful if you are planning a one-way walk and don't want the expense of a taxi pickup and drop-off. However, you'll need time, and outside of peak times you will probably need to change bus for a trip of a few hours or more. Try to pick a full bus because empty buses often trawl around the backstreets at about 3km an hour, honking and looking for customers. Tickets are purchased from an on-board conductor.

Government bus companies ply different parts of the island. The main three are the **National Transport Corporation (NTC)** (*Tel: 426 2938. www.http://ntc.intnet.mu*), **United Bus Services (UBS)** (*Tel: 212 2026*) and **Mauritius Bus Transport (MTB)**

(*Tel: 245 2539*). Regional operators are **Triolet Bus Service (TBS)** (*Tel: 261 6516*) and **Rose Hill Transport (RHT)** (*Tel: 464 1221. www.rht.mu*). In addition, private, government-regulated operators serve the island, their buses emblazoned with names as preposterous as 'Good Luck', 'Magical Mystery Tour' and 'Bad Boys'. Buses operate from 5.30am–8pm in built-up areas, and from 6.30am–6.30pm in the countryside. A bus passes the many simple bus stops throughout the island every 20 minutes. *Info Guide* (Editions Le Fleuron, 2006), sold in bookshops on the island, is full of town street maps and has excellent bus route maps, useful for independent travellers.

Hiring a vehicle

Driving is on the left here, and it's compulsory to wear a seat belt. Roads

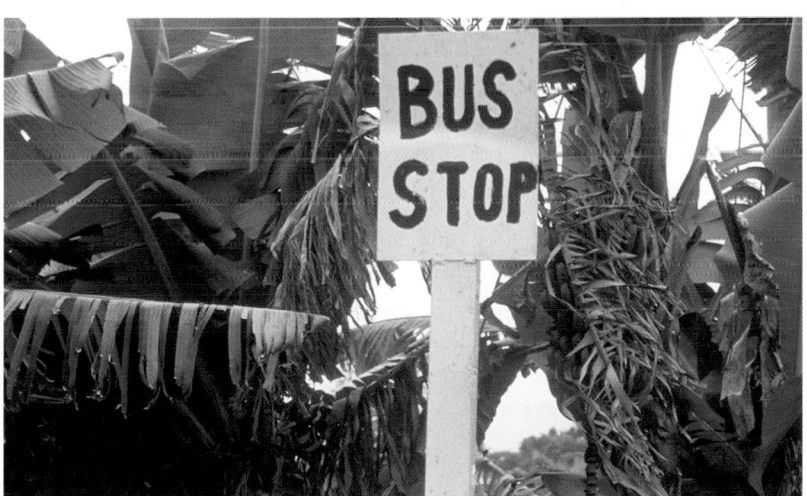

Buses are a good way of getting around remote Rodrigues Island

are often narrow, with no pavements and plenty of people and dogs. Although improving in tourist areas, towns and attractions are poorly signposted, and when usually calm, considerate and even-tempered Mauritians get behind the wheel, they can transform into impatient and erratic drivers.

Driving in Mauritius isn't for the faint-hearted, but hiring a car is still a popular, flexible and inexpensive way to tour the island. A valid driver's licence is required, and drivers must be over 23 years old. Speed limits are 80km/h (50mph) on the motorway and 50km/h (30mph) in built-up areas. Petrol is cheap, and all of the international retailers are represented here but tend to be expensive.

Car hire companies **Hertz** (*Tel: 670 4301. Email: hertz@hertzmauritius.com*), **Avis** (*Tel: 405 4200. www. avismauritius.com*) and **Sixt** (*Tel: 427 1111. www.summer-times.com*) have all the latest models, including trendy open-topped jeeps and 4WDs. If cost is a consideration and you're happy with something basic, try one of the local providers such as **ADA** (*Tel: 675 2626. www.adamaurice.net*), which will work out 25–30 per cent cheaper. All the above have offices at the airport. Motorbike hire is available from Grand Baie, organised through **Grand Baie Travel & Tours (GBTT)** (*Trou aux Biches. Tel: 265 5261. www.gbtt.com*).

Domestic flights

Air Mauritius (*Tel: 207 7070. www.airmauritius.com*) has the most frequent flights to Rodrigues, a 90-minute hop away, four times a day in peak season. Book well in advance.

Sir Seewoosagur Ramgoolam International Airport (SSR), or Plaisance Airport, as it is known, is approximately 3km (2 miles) from Mahébourg, 48km (30 miles) from Port Louis, 70km (43$^{1}/_{2}$ miles) from Grand Baie, 45km (28 miles) from Flic en Flac and 40km (25 miles) from Belle Mare. It takes from 10 to 90 minutes to drive to hotels from the airport, with an average travel time of 40 minutes. For a speedier arrival at your hotel, take a helicopter transfer.

Take care when driving – you may encounter an overloaded sugar-cane lorry like this one

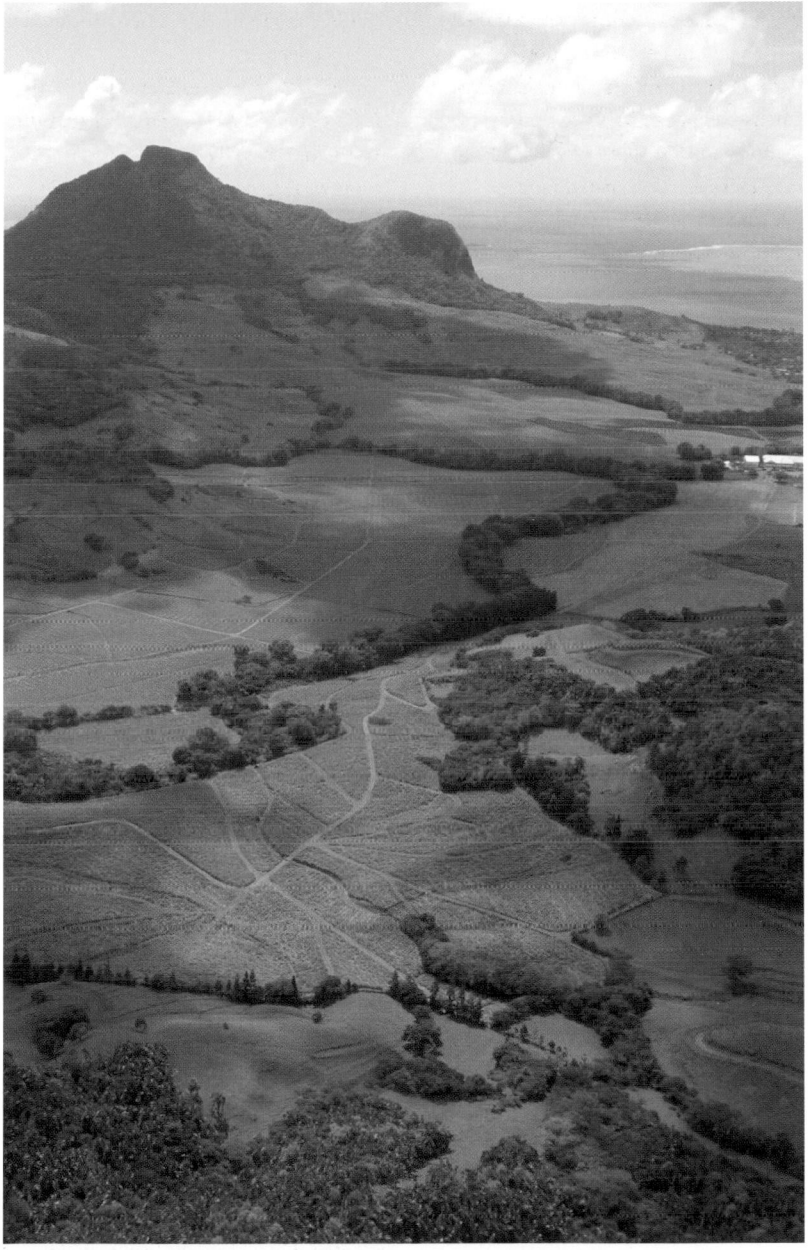

Taking a domestic flight will give you great views of Mauritius' beautiful, lush landscape

Deep-sea fishing

Mauritius is one of the best spots in the world for deep-sea fishing. The sea drops to 70m (230ft) just 1km (²⁄₃ mile) from the coast, meaning that huge fish are there for the taking 15 minutes from shore. Its tropical waters are home to blue- and black-stripe marlin, sharks, tuna, sail fish, bonitos, wahoo, dorado and the *bécune* (barracuda). The island held the world fishing record for blue marlin for 15 years and holds several other fishing records, including a 505kg (1,115lb) Mako shark, a 181kg (400lb) blue shark, a white tuna that weighed in at 102kg (224lb), a bonito of 19kg (41½lb) and a barracuda of 57kg (125lb). African records (which include Mauritius) also mention a yellow tuna of 96kg (212lb). Recently caught blue marlin weighed in at 650kg (1,430lb) and 615kg (1,355lb).

The most popular season for international anglers is from September to March, but big-game fishing is possible year-round, although it changes with the season (*see below*). Traditionally, caught fish remained the property of the boat owner, but a tag and release policy now operates from many hotels.

WHEN TO FISH FOR WHAT

Year-round – barracuda, black marlin, skipjack tuna

Mar–Apr/May – yellow-fin tuna

Sept–Dec – hammerhead shark/wahoo

Nov–Mar/Apr – sailfish, blue marlin, Mako shark.

A half or full day's boat charter can be booked through most hotels, and a number of professional fishing companies can organise boat charters for a half or full day's deep-sea fishing. Vessels are modern and well equipped

Make sure you have a record of your catch!

with radio and trolling equipment and include a knowledgeable skipper. They typically have three fighting chairs on the stern, and outriggers to troll five baits at any time designed for a maximum of six anglers. Snacks and drinks are usually provided – some even offer a barbecue on board. Being tax-free, Mauritius is also a great place to buy fishing tackle – one of the best-known shops is Quay Stores in Port Louis.

With a huge blue marlin in the clubhouse, the historic **Le Morne Anglers' Club** in Rivière Noire (*Tel: 483 5801. www.morneanglers.com*) is the only internationally recognised fishing club on the island, and a member of the International Game Fish Association (IGFA), but it's members only. This is where the prestigious **Marlin World Cup** is hosted, sponsored by Mauritius Tourism Promotion Authority (*www. marlinworldcup.com*). They also host the South Indian Ocean Billfish Competition.

Although fishing trips go out from the north and east too, it is at Flic en Flac on the west side that you can catch big fish. Here, the continental shelf drops to more than 600m (2,000ft) 1.6km (1 mile) from shore. Although in its infancy, Rodrigues Island now has a couple of companies offering deep-sea fishing charters.

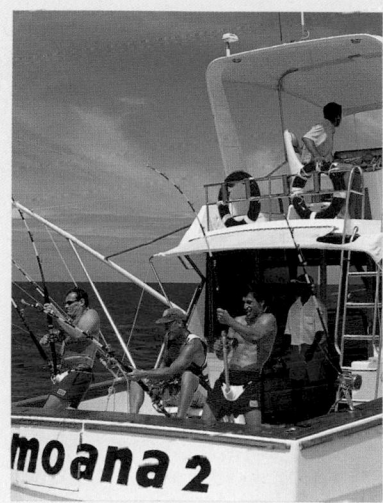
Most hotels can organise a charter

PROFESSIONAL DEEP-SEA FISHING CHARTER COMPANIES
North
Sportfisher, Grand Baie
Tel: 263 8358.
www.sportfisher.com
West
West Sails Ltd, Black River
Tel: 483 5060/728 7979 (mobile).
www.blackriver-mauritius.com
Has a contract with several hotels.
Summertimes
Big-game fishing tours (*see p101*).
Rodrigues
Rod Fishing Club
Tel: 875 0616.
www.rodfishingclub.com
East
Domaine du Pêcheur
Tel: 631 5061.

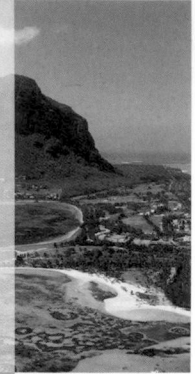

Accommodation

Mauritius has a higher density of 5-star hotels than anywhere else in the world. Think luxurious villas and colonial-style resorts with personal butlers, personal plunge pools and arrival by helicopter. Accommodation here tends to be on the expensive side, but some excellent mid-range and simple family-run hotels can be found in most areas. Moreover, an increasing number of hotels offer good-value all-inclusive packages.

There are no campsites on the island. A few interesting options exist in the interior, such as staying in old colonial mansions or lodges, almost all associated with a Domaine or ecotourism offering. Other options include private *campements* or 'weekend houses' to rent island-wide, apartments, villas and beach bungalows called *pieds dans l'eau* (feet in the water) by the locals. There are also *chambres d'hôtes* (bed and breakfasts), some at very competitive prices. In addition to the recent development of the untamed southwest at Bel Ombre, boutique hotels and villa developments are blossoming.

Hotels

Five main hotel groups operate here: Beachcomber, Kerzner International – One&Only Resorts, Naiade Resorts, Constance Hotels and Veranda Resorts. The well-known international chains such as Hilton, Oberoi, Four Seasons, Méridien, Taj and Intercontinental can

also be found, plus, new for 2011, St Regis. What distinguishes Mauritian hotels is the value and high level of service. Even in 3- or 4-star hotels, the service is better than on other tropical islands and is certainly the best in the Indian Ocean. Over 100 hotels and resorts are dotted around the island, nearly all overlooking the island's white-sand beaches, and offering the ingredients of a holiday from heaven, from kids' clubs to golf, and from spa treatments to every watersport imaginable.

Each region of the island has a slightly different vibe and landscape, offers varied activities, and lies near different attractions, so it's worth considering what you want from your Mauritian holiday before booking accommodation. Picking up a Tourist Information Guide from offices will help with research. If you're mainly interested in watersports, it would make sense to stay near Grand Baie or the east coast. If you have small children, the west coast has some of the safest beaches. For nightlife, head to

Grand Baie in the north, but for tranquillity, try Le Morne or Bel Ombre in the quieter southwest. Mauritius is small, but bear in mind that it takes time to travel between regions when choosing accommodation.

Self-catering

Self-catering accommodation is mostly concentrated in tourist areas with facilities such as Grand Baie, north of Belle Mare in the east, and in the west around Flic en Flac. However,

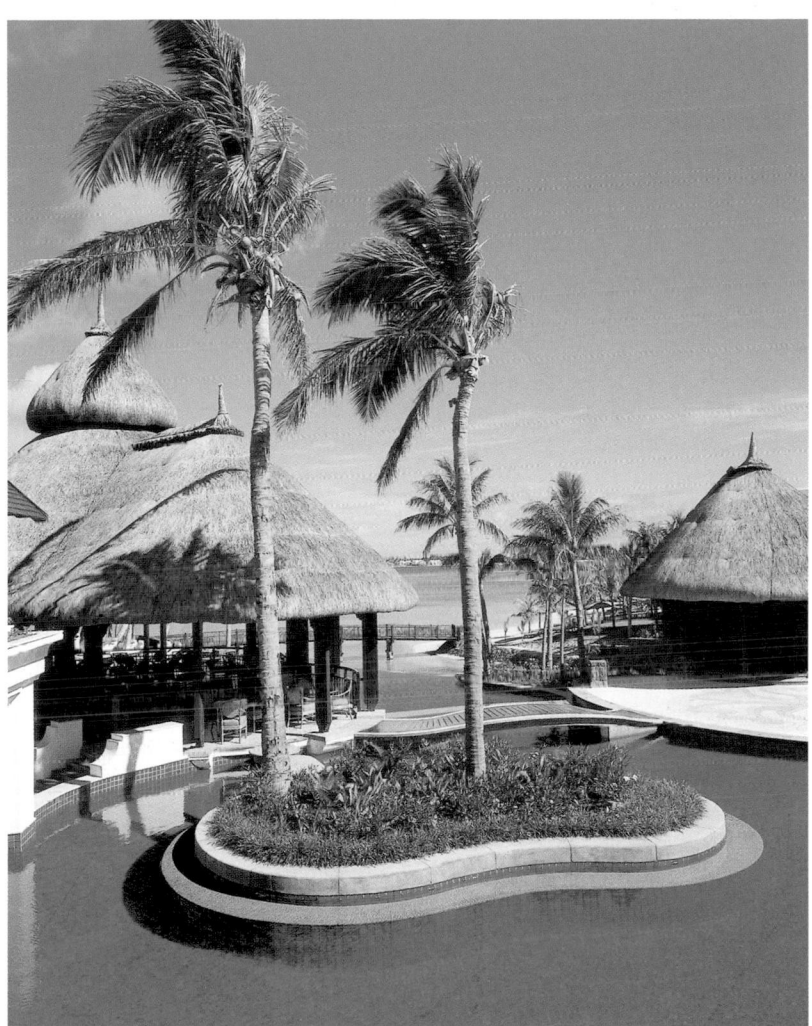

The main pool at Le Touessrok resort, Trou d'Eau Douce

CELEBRITY SPOTTING

Anyone who is anyone has stayed on Mauritius. Prince William is a regular at One&Only Le Saint Géran, where Sharon Stone, Geri Halliwell and John Travolta have also stayed. The likes of Joseph Fiennes and Naomi Campbell have stayed in its sister hotel, One&Only Le Touessrok. J K Rowling appeared at the Residence, Jade Jagger at the Oberoi, and Michael Douglas and Catherine Zeta Jones were spotted at perhaps the poshest hotel on the island, Le Prince Maurice.

there are options islandwide if you know where to look. They range from basic concrete blocks at a bargain price to exclusive villas with a butler and prices to match. Once only found through word of mouth, they now advertise and accept bookings over the Internet.

Villa or beach bungalows

Villas de Maitre

(*www.villasdemaitre.com*) has a good selection of villas and beach bungalows around the island, including 40 luxury villas near the golf course at Bel Ombre. **Elegant Destinations** (*Tel: 0870 8908877 (UK). www.elegant destinations.co.uk*) offer over 200 beach villas and eco villas. An array of tempting apartments can be found at *www.mauritius-islander.com* and **Mauritius Individuell** (*www.mauritius-individuell.com*).

Typical offerings by small outfits include **Seapoint Beach Bungalows** (*Tel: 696 4804. www.seapoint bungalows.com*) with studios, apartments and beach bungalows at Pointe aux Canonniers, Grand Baie; the budget studios and apartments offered

You can stay in a colonial-style house, such as this one in Le Saint Aubin

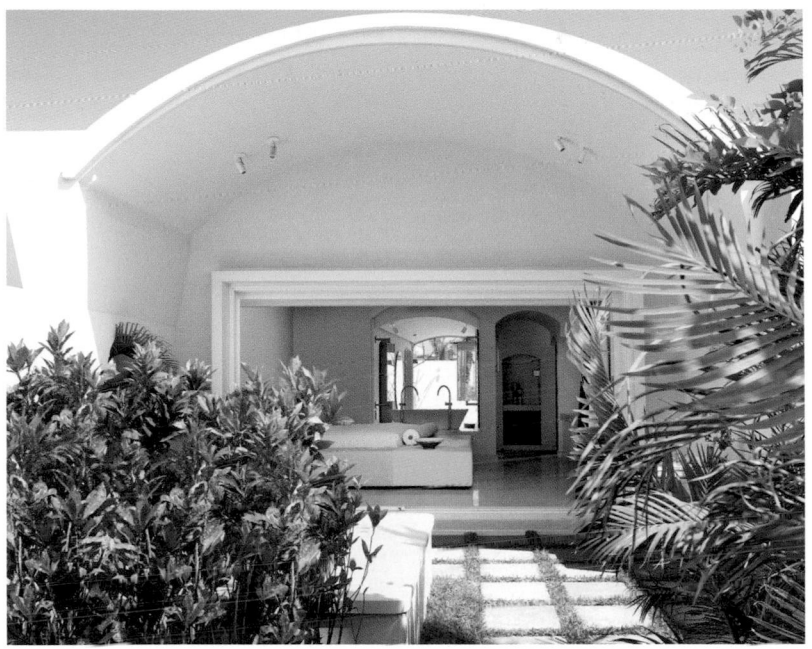

One of the villas with private gardens at So Mauritius

by **Pingouinvillas** (*Tel: 637 3051. www.pingouinvillas.com*) near Blue Bay; cheap, clean and cheerful Art Deco apartments offered by **Residence Art** (*Tel: 453 5277*) on Royal Road, Flic en Flac; and **Les Lataniers Bleus** (*Tel: 483 6541. http://leslataniersbleus.com*) with three pretty, blue villas around a swimming pool next to the beach in Black River village.

Eco options include reasonably priced, private rustic lodges made out of stone and thatch, owned by Lodges d'Union: **L'Exil**, inland from the south coast, and **Les Lodges d'Andrea**, in a pretty spot at Rivière des Anguilles, near Gris Gris (*Tel both lodges: 471 0555. www.relaisdeslodges.com*).

A renovated private villa on a peninsula can be found with **Yemaya Shores** (*Tel: 288 8189, www.yemayashores.com*). **Les Chalets Verangue** (*Coeur Bois, near Le Morne. Tel: 290 6688*), attached to Le Verangue sur Morne restaurant (*see p155*), is an unusual choice, nestled privately in the forest below Plaine Champagne.

SPECIAL INTERESTS

Want to see if your hotel has a kids' club, spa, nightclub, casino or dive centre? Fancy kite-surfing, golf or deep-sea fishing, or finding the best places to shop? Consult the Activity Planner and handy Interactive Map at **Mauritius Tourism Promotion Authority (MTPA)** (*www.tourism-mauritius.mu*).

A taste of Mauritius

Eating in Mauritius is a great pleasure as the cuisine is as interesting as it is varied, with a collision of world culinary traditions that has created something unique. The island's hotels serve plenty of exotic seafood dishes, including *camarons* (freshwater crayfish), giant prawns and freshly harvested oysters. Venison and wild boar have made it on to menus from French hunting traditions on the island, and palm hearts or 'millionaire's salads' are often served with smoked blue marlin, another speciality here. The Creole influence is rich in tomatoes, onions, ginger, garlic and chillies, such as in *rougaille* (an African spicy tomato paste). Other traditional dishes include *daube* (beef or chicken stew), *vindaye* (deep-fried fish coated in turmeric, ginger, chillies and mustard seeds), *snoeck rougaille* (salted fish in traditional tomato sauce), *kalya* (meat or fish cooked with saffron and garlic or ginger), and the use of *chevrettes* (freshwater shrimp) and *tec-tec* (clams).

There's plenty of fresh fruit grown on the island, with *litchis* (lychees), mangoes, pineapples, papaya and

Chillies drying in the sun – a much-used ingredient in Mauritius

bananas found on street stalls or in the island's markets, and definitely on your breakfast table. Mauritians don't typically eat out much, but they munch on *gajaks* (snacks) all day and buy lunch out. To find local specialities, leave your hotel and take your cue from the office workers – follow them to food stalls and sit in the park, or go to one of the scruffy-looking but popular eateries.

Street food

It's easy and usually safe to try street food in Mauritius – mostly of an Indian and African flavour with a dash of French. You'll find carts or bicycles, with a glass case on the back, parked on town streets, markets or even in backyards all over the island, selling mainly Indian specialities including *dholl purri* (a soft, savoury pancake stuffed with mashed split peas and *rougaille*), *roti* (pancakes filled with meat and potato curry) and *samosas* (deep-fried pastry pockets stuffed with curried vegetables). Vans sometimes specialise in one dish such as *gateaux piments* (deep-fried chilli and split pea cakes). The street vendors in larger towns such as Port Louis, Curepipe, Quatre Bornes and Grand Baie often offer the traditional Creole accompaniments, *rougaille* or *achard* (shredded carrots, cabbage, beans and cauliflower cooked al

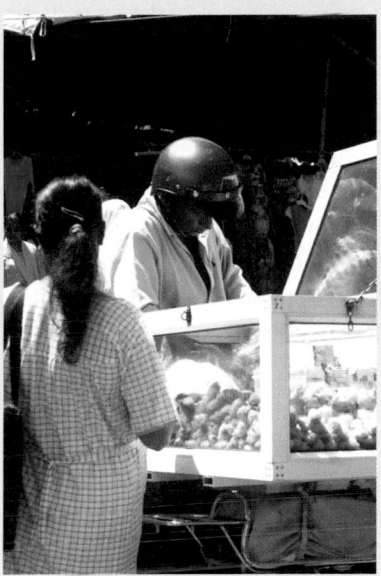

A *gajak* seller in Mahébourg

dente with garlic and onions). Port Louis has the highest concentration of street vendors selling Chinese noodles and broths, and in Chinatown you'll find glass cases full of Chinese cakes.

The Muslim's contribution to Mauritian cuisine is *briani* or *halim* (a thick soup of mutton, lentils and rice) as well as halal kebabs. Hawkers in towns and often beside public beaches at weekends serve these, and some open late into the evening.

Stalls sell pineapple peeled and carved into a spiral, which makes a refreshing snack. Fresh King Coconut juice can be found in towns, at tourist attractions and beside public beaches alongside Western fast food.

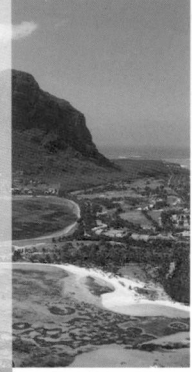

Food and drink

The cuisine in Mauritius reflects the diversity of its multicultural people, whose ancestors came from countries with strong culinary traditions – France, India and China. Eating in Mauritius is exciting – where else could you eat fresh baguettes for breakfast and octopus vindaloo for dinner? The Chinese eat curry, Indians have fried rice and, traditionally, Franco-Mauritians have rice and Creole specialities at midday, and a European-style dinner.

Dining out

Dining out can be as casual or glitzy as you wish. Fabulous value-for-money Chinese, French and Indian restaurants are dotted around every town, although Grand Baie has the highest concentration, along with international restaurants such as Japanese and Italian. Lunch can be savoured with table d'hôte Creole specialities in an increasing array of rustic restaurants in the south. Alternatively, enjoy lunch or dinner in an elegant setting at one of the Domaines, with lovely locations on

If you don't want a full meal, pick up a cooked-to-order snack at a stall

the old sugar plantations around the island, serving mainly Creole classics with a French twist. At hotels, there's everything from dining à la carte by candlelight beside the beach to casual beach barbecues. For a really special evening meal, Mauritius' 5-star hotels are home to top restaurants. Spoon des Îles at One&Only Le Saint Géran is the first Alain Ducasse restaurant to set up outside France. And one of the newest, Origine at Amahita, is a gourmet restaurant run by Michelin-starred chef Jean-Pierre Vigato.

Fish-eaters will have a ball here, with plenty of seafood to choose from. However, vegetarians may find it difficult to find a staple protein as cheese and eggs don't abound outside hotels, but there are plenty of vegetable curries, bean dishes, varied salads and fresh fruit at hand.

Local tipples

The local tipple is rum, made from the sugar cane grown across the island Green Island Rum is the most famous and often mixed with fruit juice to create delicious rum cocktails. Perhaps more interesting, however, are the agricultural rums made from the first pressing of the sugar cane on some Domaines such as the new Rhumerie de Chamarel, as well as in homes. These are often combined with the vanilla grown on Mauritius, or steeped with local fruit.

Mauritius produces some award-winning and therefore very drinkable

beers. Phoenix, the oldest and main brewery on the island, produces two lagers: Phoenix, referred to in Creole as 'spider beer' because the label looks like one, and the slightly stronger, at 6 per cent, Blue Marlin. Otherwise, there's the higher proof Black Eagle lager, produced by a newer, Indian brewery. It may surprise you to discover that Mauritius also makes its own wines, the Oxenham range, although the grape is imported. Try Eureka or, if you want to go more upmarket, something bearing the St Nicholas label. Whisky is the preferred Mauritian tipple, but it is expensive here.

Local soft drinks to try include tamarind juice and *alooda*, a sweet milky drink with black falooda seeds that swell up like sago, flavoured with rose syrup and sweet basil.

Tipping

Many restaurants include a service charge, but the waiting staff still expect a tip. Most people leave some change or up to 10 per cent of the bill. Cafés and pubs in more touristy areas also expect a tip, but it's not compulsory to leave one.

Food and drink

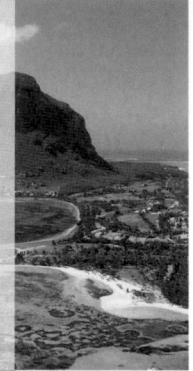

Entertainment

Mauritius is not the place for a raucous holiday. As the hotels are mainly on the coast or isolated inland, away from the towns, entertainment tends to be hotel-based. The larger resorts offer everything from cabaret shows and discos to intimate dining, soft piano bars and weekly Sega dancing performances.

There are some excellent restaurants in the Caudan Waterfront in Port Louis that are attractively lit up at night. Other than this, the liveliest nightlife is found at Flic en Flac and Grand Baie on a Friday and Saturday night. Flic en Flac is inexpensive, but it's really only Grand Baie that is buzzing in the evening. Grand Baie has a variety of nightlife, from trendy bars to the widest range of international restaurants and several nightclubs. Nightclubs often charge a small entrance fee, although women sometimes get in free.

Mauritius is also not a place to get cultural. It's too far from anywhere to attract more than the occasional international artist or performer. The main cinema, with three screens and showing English-language films, is at the Caudan Waterfront in Port Louis. There are also cinemas in Rose Hill, Curepipe and Mahébourg, although the films tend to be dubbed into French. There are two theatres on the island, one in Port Louis and one in Rose Hill.

'What's on' listings can be found in *Islandinfo*, a free monthly magazine with an up-to-date online version (*www.islandinfo.mu*). There are casinos in Curepipe, Domaine Les Pailles and Port Louis that attract a mix of locals and tourists to the slot machines (open in the early evening) and tables (open at 9pm Monday to Saturday and 3pm on Sundays). They are also found in Trou aux Biches, One&Only Le Saint Géran, La Pirogue and Berjaya Le Morne hotels.

As for daytime entertainment, there are a few good museums, but it tends to focus on shopping centres, some of which sport art galleries, and French-style cafés frequented by both tourists and locals. Local culture is best experienced in the street life and annual religious festivals.

Mauritians don't tend to dine out in restaurants much in the evening, eating their main meal at home. Instead, they congregate around snack stalls on public beaches on Saturday nights, the men with their guitars poised ready for some Sega. Other than that, you may be lucky and catch an Indian wedding, when the whole extended family gathers to celebrate, with traditional food eaten from banana leaves, using the fingers.

Places to meet both locals and expats are Rotary Clubs in the main towns and Lions Clubs in Port Louis, Quatre Bornes and Curepipe. Golfing guests are able to visit the inexpensive bar and restaurant at the Gymkhana Club, where Thursday night is darts night. Experienced divers can obtain temporary membership of the Mauritius Underwater Group (MUG) club and join their clubhouse BYO BBQ on Tuesday nights. Anyone can join a friendly crowd of expats and locals at the Hash House Harriers, the 'drinking club with a running problem', which meets every second Sunday morning in off-the-beaten-track spots around the island (*www.mhash.com*). A nominal fee includes a run, drinks and lunch.

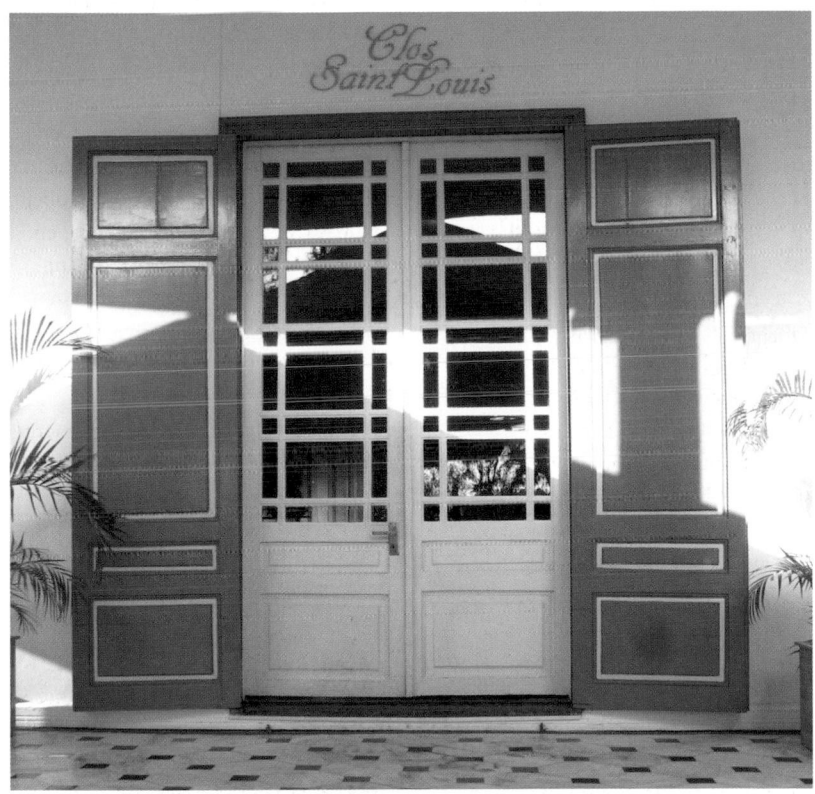

Dine at an elegant restaurant such as Clos Saint Louis, Domaine Les Pailles

Honeymoons on Mauritius

Mauritius is one of the world's top five hotspots for honeymoons and weddings. Couples have an incredible choice of over 100 mainly 5- and 4-star resorts hugging the coast, most overlooking the island's white-sand beaches. Then there are the top-quality spas, gourmet cuisine, tropical climate and excellent service. Unlike other tropical island destinations, there's a lot to see and do here, from hiking around impressive volcanic peaks in the interior to diving on the coral reef circling the island.

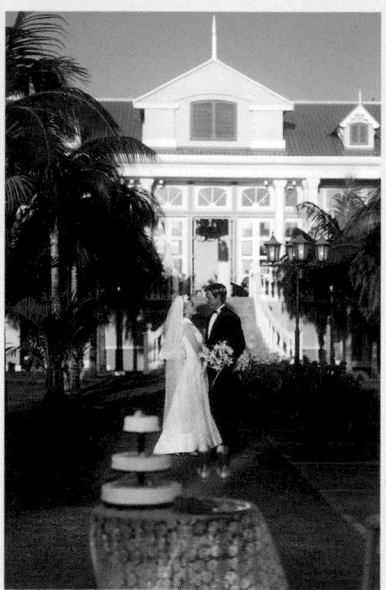

Mauritius makes an idyllic wedding setting

Honeymoon packages may include gifts, flowers and fruit, dinner, or a spa treatment.

Five hotels made for honeymooners

Dinarobin Hotel Golf & Spa

Between the dramatic Le Morne Brabant and a white-sand beach, this 172-suite hotel is in one of the best spots on the island. It has a stunning infinity pool, sumptuous Clarins Spa with saunas, Turkish baths, Jacuzzi®, an 18-hole golf course and a beach gazebo for a romantic wedding.
www.dinarobin-hotel.com

Hilton Mauritius Resort & Spa

A big resort, this suits couples who don't want to hide away, and who like activities – think horse riding, mountain biking and free watersports. The 193 rooms are sea-facing, light and airy, and there are four restaurants and nightly entertainment.
www.hilton.co.uk/mauritius

Maradiva Villas Resort & Spa

This hotel's 65 luxurious and spacious villas are exquisite. Each is private with its own plunge pool. Inside are a giant bed, polished wood floors and exquisite furnishings. The bathrooms

are the most romantic on the island.
The little extras, 24-hour butler service
and mouthwatering Mediterranean
cuisine on a candlelit jetty, all add up
to extreme pampering.
www.maradiva.com

Oberoi Mauritius

This stunning 5-star deluxe hotel
with 73 villas and 6 pavilions is by
Turtle Bay on the northwest coast.
The unusual architecture, amazing
swimming pool, wonderful service
and tasteful Eastern-inspired décor are
complemented by Mauritian sugar-
cane thatch roofs, volcanic boulders
and tropical plants. A honeymoon
highlight is a private sunset
catamaran cruise.
www.oberoihotels.com

Honeymoon in style at an idyllic resort

The Residence

An elegant plantation-style resort that
serves afternoon tea on the veranda
under elegant ceiling fans. The 163
rooms and suites are tastefully
decorated with four-poster beds and
cool tiled floors, and have views over
a white-sand beach and turquoise
lagoon. Private butlers, three
restaurants and the Sanctuary Spa
make it a haven.
www.theresidence.com

Dream weddings

Civil and religious weddings in
Mauritius are recognised in the UK.

For civil weddings, couples need to
visit the Registrar's office 24 hours in
advance, but for religious weddings,
couples must be on the island for
15 days before the ceremony – time
to work on that tan.

Most hotels have a coordinator to
organise a tailor-made dream
wedding. If you don't fancy a beach
wedding, you could arrive by
helicopter or get married underwater
with Blue Safari Submarine (*see
pp38–9*). Hotels offer special
wedding packages and, unlike
some countries, weddings here are
limited to one a day.

Shopping

Like other activities on Mauritius, shopping is a multicultural experience. Pretty French-designed sundresses sit alongside African sculptures and drums, colourful Indian saris and religious art. The jewellery-making techniques brought by Indian and Arabian immigrants are still used, and the making of model ships evolved out of the melting pot.

WHAT TO BUY

Mauritius is one of the largest textile exporters in the world, supplying clothes for major international chains and designer labels. Holiday bargains include cashmere and traditional arts and crafts in the shopping arcades; sunglasses and jewellery in duty-free shops; and Indian bedspreads, spices, leatherwork and colourful baskets in the markets.

High-street brands and designer clothing exported to Europe originate in Mauritius, and seconds can be picked up in factory shops around the island. High-quality cotton, silk and linen clothes are found for bargain prices in shopping centres. Children's clothing is available through a number of retailers – Gecko Kids, Pomme d'Api and Tara offer a wide selection of garments for newborns to teenagers. Quality knitwear is a good buy here – cashmere, a speciality, costs a third of the price in the West. Mauritius is also known for handmade tailored suits, delivered within 24–72 hours (try *New Bombay Trading. Rose Hill. Tel: 464 0948,*

www.singlepartner.mu). For interesting designs, try Shibani, which has an outlet near the **Floréal Knitwear Shop** in Floréal (*Tel: 601 1000*), said to be one of the best places to buy cashmere sweaters in the centre of the island. It also has shops in the Caudan, Grand Baie and Flic en Flac.

Perfume, jewellery and electrical goods can be purchased for discount prices in duty-free shops. Bright straw bags made here, *pareos* (sarongs), cotton T-shirts and imported Indian embroidered cushion covers are also good, inexpensive buys. Model ships are a unique local craft. Then there are the souvenirs – local rum and vanilla tea, spices, smoked marlin, anthurium flowers (the red flowers with yellow middles often seen in hotel decorations) and Sega CDs. And, of course, a miniature dodo.

Glassware

At the **Mauritius Glass Gallery** in Phoenix, watch artisans blow recycled glass into objects as varied as lamps, vases and dodos. Buy direct from the workshop or from shops at the Caudan Craft Market.

Mauritius Glass Gallery, Pont Fer, Phoenix. Tel: 696 3360. www.mauritiusglassgallery.mu. Open: Mon–Fri 8.30am–4.30pm, Sat 8.30am–noon. Closed: Sun. Admission charge.

Model ships

Around 40 years ago, Jose Ramar made a model ship for fun. Someone from the first French Embassy saw it and took it to France. There was much demand there for models, and the embassy helped with the plans for famous ships such as the *Victory, Bounty* and *Le Saint-Géran.* Mauritius has since built a reputation for the art and craft of building miniature copies of famous ships, with about 60 models to choose from. Built to the scale of the original plan, with every detail perfectly reproduced, the ships are made of teak or mahogany, with the sails usually dipped in tea to give them that ancient look. Shops will send your purchase for you, or pack it well to carry on or put in the hold, but airlines may charge for carriage according to size and weight.

Workshops around the island are open to visitors, and ships can be bought on-site:

Historic Marine Factory

Goodlands. Tel: 283 9304. www.historic-marine.com. Open: Mon–Fri 8.30am–5pm; Sat & Sun 9am–1pm.

Bags for sale at an arts and crafts market in Port Louis

First Fleet Reproduction

Phoenix. Tel: 698 0161. www.firstfleet reproductions.com. Open: Mon–Fri 9am–5pm. Closed: Sat & Sun.

WHERE TO BUY

Shopping excursions from hotels usually include factory outlets, duty-free shops and tourist shopping arcades, and typically focus on Grand Baie, Port Louis and sometimes Curepipe. For a more local and personalised experience, hire a taxi to take you around.

Duty-free shops

The sign 'Duty Free' appears on many shops, but in the official outlets there's a certain procedure. The main shops with this facility are jewellers, such as Adamas duty-free diamond boutique for fine-cut gems, Shiv jewels, designer clothes shops, electronics shops and, for handmade items, Ravior and Charles Lee. However, new shopping

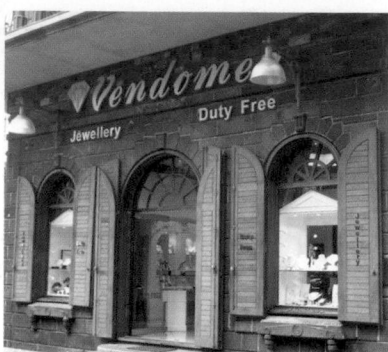

Duty-free jewellery shopping at Caudan Waterfront

centres continue to spring up around the island.

The tax rebate on these goods used to be around 40 per cent, but now up to 2,000 items have an 80 per cent tax rebate. Hazara, the carpet dealers who pack and send purchases by air freight, take 100 per cent of the tax off.

There are two ways to buy duty-free goods. Either way requires payment in foreign currency, and showing your passport and ongoing/return air ticket. Traditionally, the tax is taken off goods and they're delivered to the airport to collect on departure. If you'd rather take your goods away with you, and you are shopping less than 48 hours before departure, if you pay the full price at the time of purchase you can claim a rebate (in the same currency) at the airport.

North
Port Louis
If you can only make one shopping trip, it should be to the capital, Port Louis. Here, air-conditioned malls at the Caudan Waterfront lie opposite the sprawling Central Market, factory outlets rub shoulders with small boutiques selling Indian saris, and street sellers line the cracked pavements selling everything from chickens to cheap Western clothing.

Caudan Waterfront
The best loved of shopping centres in Mauritius, 'The Caudan', as it's affectionately known, is the island's most glamorous shopping centre. The original building has 60 shops, including branches of all the well-known outlets and duty-free shops, with another 55 shops in Dias Pier. Probably the greatest attraction is the range of gifts from paintings to spices in its traditional arts and crafts market, where crafts such as basket-weaving can be seen. The Caudan doubles as a leisure centre with art galleries, a museum, bars, restaurants, a three-screen cinema, and even a casino housed in a replica of a pirate ship. *Old Pavillon Street, Le Caudan. Tel: 211 6560 for the information kiosk. www.caudan.com. Open: Mon–Sat 9.30am–5.30pm, Sun 9.30am–noon. Sales Oct & May.*

PROTECT THE REEFS
Try to avoid buying coral and shells. The government is trying to crack down on people taking these from Mauritius' reefs. Although many are now imported, this just means that another country's reef is being destroyed.

BE ON YOUR GUARD

Watch out for taxis who try to take you to shops where they get commission. This is a common scam in Mauritius – and you end up paying for it.

Grand Baie

Grand Baie's Sunset Boulevard on Royal Road is an extensive open-air arcade, right next to the shore. Full of upmarket jewellery, crafts and clothing boutiques, it is a good place for *pareos* (sarongs) and designer surfwear, at great prices. It has some unusual shops such as **Vaco Art Gallery** (*Dodo Square. Tel: 263 3106. www.vacoartiste.com. Open: Mon Sat 9.30am 7pm. Closed: Sun*), hung with colourful and tropical paintings by Vaco Baissac, one of the island's best-known artists.

Central Mauritius

Factory outlets selling goods such as Ralph Lauren and Levi's seconds at

Indian textiles on sale in Flic en Flac

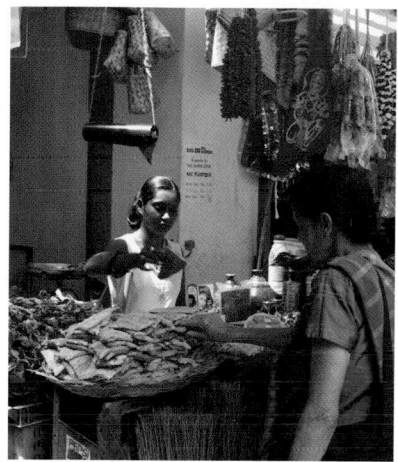
Mahébourg market

discount prices are found mainly in the inland towns, where 30 per cent of the population lives. If you have time to poke around, the little Chinese and Indian shops, and the shopping arcades in Rose Hill, Quatre Bornes and Curepipe are the places to find similar goods at half the price of tourist shopping centres. Try the well-established Sunnassee Arcade in Rose Hill, the Orchard Centre in Quatre Bornes, Currimgee, Salafa (good for jeans) and Yanpalach in Curepipe.

Islandwide

Tourist shopping centres, such as Garden Village in Curepipe, are springing up around the island. **Ruisseau Créole** (*Tel: 483 8000. http://ruisseaucreole.com. Open: Mon–Sat 9.30am–6.30pm. Closed: Sun*) is a good one on the main road between Tamarin and Black River.

ISLANDWIDE MARKETS

A Mauritian shopping experience has to include a trip to one of its traditional and colourful markets in order to practise the national sport of bargaining. Expect to pay about a third of the price proposed. Start by offering a quarter until you both come to a compromise. If the stall holder still doesn't bite, try walking away – it often works. Many stalls move from place to place on different days, but each market has its own character and flavour. Apart from in Port Louis, most markets start early and close by 4pm.

Central Market, Port Louis

At the craft market upstairs, squeeze through alleys of sequinned shoes and gypsy skirts, pashminas, Indian bags, cushion covers and bedspreads, *pareos* (sarongs) and fake designer T-shirts. There's a good selection of gifts, but bargain hard. (*See also pp27–9.*)
Between Queen and Farquhar streets.
Open: Mon–Fri 6am–6pm, Sat 6am–noon.

Flacq market

Although this is the largest outdoor market on the island, and fun to visit

HAWKERS

If you can't be bothered to go into towns to pick up a few souvenirs and would rather lie on your hotel beach with a cool drink and refreshing swim nearby, don't worry, the shops will come to you. Hawkers are permitted on most of the hotel beaches and sell jewellery, *pareos* (sarongs) and other items. If you're not interested, they'll just move on.

for its atmosphere, it mainly sells fruit, vegetables and other foodstuffs, rather than bargain souvenirs.
La Source Street, near the stadium.
Open: Wed & Sun.

Goodlands Market

In the north, this market is smaller and less touristy than some others.
New Grand Gaube. Open: Tue & Fri.

Mahébourg market

Situated around the bus station and stretching to the waterfront, this is perhaps the most traditional market, and the least visited by tourists. It has all the usual Chinese and Western clothing, and a great one-stop souvenir stall, **La Croisée Balance** (*opposite Monte Carlo. Tel: 637 9766*), selling a variety of baskets, picture frames, dodos and so on for the cheapest prices.
Mahébourg Waterfront. Open: Mon.

Quatre Bornes market

Perhaps the second most popular market with tourists, this specialises in textiles. It is the place locals go for material such as silk, cotton and linen.

The market also sells export-quality seconds, at very attractive prices, with jeans a particularly good buy.

Stalls are conveniently situated in the town centre. Open: Thur & Sun from around 8am–4pm.

The Central Market in Port Louis

Sport and leisure

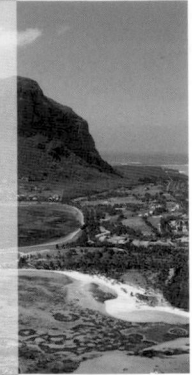

Just about everyone in Mauritius is mad about English football. If you want to strike up a conversation with a local lad, try talking Man United or Liverpool. He'll probably be wearing one of the shirts to give you a clue. You'll find this national sport played everywhere from stadiums to scruffy patches of dirt between the filao trees.

SPECTATOR SPORTS
Horse racing

Weekends between May and November see both tourists and locals form crowds of up to 30,000 to watch international jockeys at Champ de Mars racecourse in Port Louis. The Mauritius Derby is the main event on the calendar, held at the end of August. Check details on *www.mauritiusturfclub.com*

PARTICIPATION SPORTS
Cross-country running

The Mauritius marathon happens in June (*www.mauritiusmarathon.com*).

The Royal Raid, a cross-country mountain marathon, started in Mauritius in 2006, is now an annual event, taking international runners 35km (22 miles) across the island every spring (*www.royalraid.com*).

Cycling

Bicycles can be hired for just an hour or up to a day from major hotels and from some agencies in the north. Some hotels, particularly in the quieter southwest, offer cycle trails, but most cycling is done as a guided tour. The best cycling experience is to get out into nature, with Beachcomber through their hotels or, better still, with specialist Yemaya Adventures, which offers bicycle day trips as well as cycling holidays (*see p151*).

Golf

A choice of at least eight 18-hole golf courses and five 9-hole courses on the island, and growing, makes Mauritius a serious golfing destination. With courses set among the world's most beautiful hotels with stunning scenery to match, it's an inspiring place for a game. Most courses are in upmarket hotels, used by residents for no charge, but with a green fee for non-residents. Many hotels require non-residents to book tee-off times, and many offer professional instruction. The most celebrated are in the east and southwest

of the island, although there are clubs in every region. The Bernard Langer-designed 18-hole golf course on Île aux Cerfs must be one of the world's greatest golf settings, and you can even arrive by helicopter.
www.mauritiusgolfcollection.co.uk

Hiking/trekking

Most hiking trails in Mauritius lie in the Black River Gorges National Park on Plaine Champagne, where hikes vary from half an hour to a full day, and from easy to strenuous. Hiking is also offered on private land in the Domaines, which have opened up as ecotourism parks (*see pp96–7*), and on Mauritius' mountains (*see pp70–71*). The most popular mountain hike is up the thumb-shaped Le Pouce (*see pp44–5*), suitable for the whole family. Others, such as Le Morne or Lion Mountain, are technical in parts and should not be undertaken without a guide.

Horse riding

Horse riding is best done in the morning or late afternoon to avoid the heat of the day. Many hotels can arrange horse riding, with stables scattered along the coast, although standards and safety vary considerably. Excursions are offered by the few professional stables on the island, and at some Domaines.

Watersports

Mauritius is a mecca for watersports enthusiasts. It offers waterskiing, sailing, windsurfing, kite-surfing, sea-kayaking and parasailing as well as

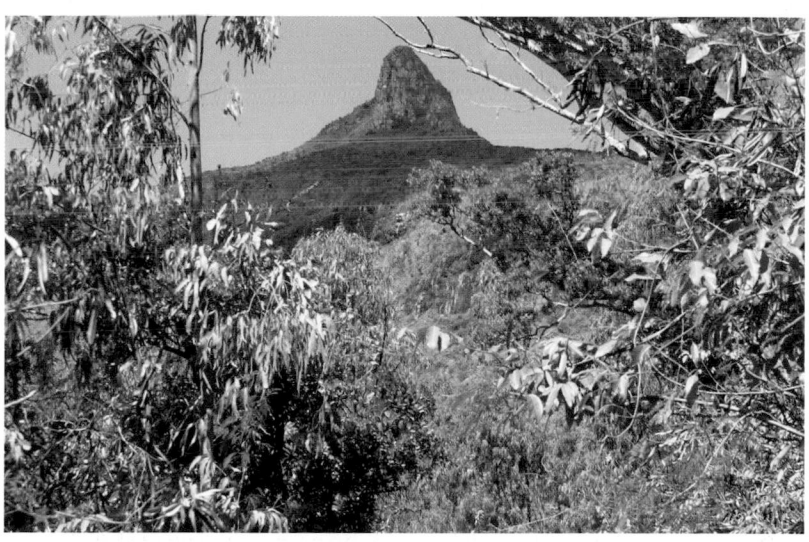

Many visitors tackle the hike to Le Pouce from Port Louis

first-class diving and snorkelling around the island. Plastic or sailing shoes should be worn as a precaution against getting cut on sharp coral, or stepping on stonefish, depending on what activity you're doing.

Deep-sea fishing
See pp112–13.

Diving
See pp86–7.

Kayaking
The two places for sea-kayaking in Mauritius are up the Grande Rivière Sud-Est (Southeast) on the east coast to see a waterfall, and half- or full-day trips around the more isolated Île d'Ambre (Amber Island) in the north (*see p103*), in addition to offerings by hotels.

Parasailing
This is a popular sport on the island and soars up to 200m (650ft) from Grand Baie.

Pirogue Regatta
This is a three-day race in the historic southeast during the second week of December. Either be in it, combining a stay with eco-activities in Mauritius, or be a spectator. For more information, *tel: 622 7234 or 422 3117 (mobile). www.laregatta.com*

Sailing
The calm waters of the lagoon make Mauritius a good spot for sailing, and its epicentre is Grand Baie. Small dinghies are available at the large beach hotels or you can charter a catamaran from Rivière Noire in the west or Île aux Cerfs in the east with **White Sand**

Try the latest activity, parasailing, at Grand Baie

Le Morne is one of the best locations for windsurfing and kite-surfing

Tours (*Tel: 212 3712, www.whitesand tours.com*). Catamaran cruises are popular, and are organised by many hotels and Summertimes (*see p102*). They are usually a full day including lunch and snorkelling. The most popular cruises are to the Northern Islands or to see dolphins in Tamarin Bay.

Snorkelling

The coral gardens of Mauritius are some of the best in the Indian Ocean, and opportunities for snorkelling abound all around the island. Snorkelling gear is usually complimentary from hotels, or it can be rented from dive centres or picked up cheaply from stalls and supermarkets in tourist areas. The best underwater scenery for snorkellers is found at Blue Bay Marine Park, Le Morne, Flic en Flac on the west coast, and Trou aux Biches and Turtle Bay marine park in the north.

Waterskiing

The lagoons of Mauritius make great waterskiing spots. This is offered free of charge for residents in more upmarket hotels and for a fee at many mid-range establishments.

Windsurfing and kite-surfing

Mauritius has long been a favourite for windsurfers, particularly the windier east coast. But it's now also a hotspot for kite-surfing, with Le Morne cited as one of the best sites in the world.

There are five main kite-surfing schools here, all **IKO (International Kiteboarding Organization**; *www.ikointl.com*) certified. Kite-surfing outfits are also found in Cap Malheureux and Grand Gaube in the north, and at Pointe d'Esny and Belle Mare in the east. Spots and schools can be found at *www.mauritiusurf.com*

Spas

Mauritius can now provide a holiday for mind, body and soul in its top-quality spas, boasting a wide range of treatments and therapies from all over the world. Most hotels and resorts have luxurious spas with everything from Ayurvedic treatments based on Indian and Creole remedies sourced from local herbs and flowers to ocean-inspired treatments and exclusive products from top beauty brands and fashion houses such as Clarins, Givenchy and Shiseido.

The island's leading spas are at One&Only Le Saint Géran, Paradise Cove, Legends, The Royal Palm, The Hilton, Le Prince Maurice, Beau Rivage, The Oberoi, The Residence, Belle Mare Plage, Dinarobin, Heritage Awali Golf & Spa Resort, Heritage Le Telfair, The Four Seasons and The Indian Resort. Some of these are open to non-residents, although you should book ahead.

FIVE TOP-CLASS SPA PICKS
Givenchy at Le Touessrok

One of the few Givenchy spas in the world, this is found at Le Touessrok (*see p156*). Choose from peels, wraps, jets, stones and electrotherapy to help with weight loss, body and skin conditioning, or try the four hands (two therapists) Ylang Ylang massage for a trip to paradise.
www.letouessrokresort.com

The Sanctuary, The Residence

This nine-room spa with soft cream furnishings offers treatments from exclusive Swiss cosmetic brand La Prairie. Try the WellSun treatment that combines steam bath, gentle exfoliation with sand and essential oils, and a gentle massage, to prepare your skin for tanning.
www.theresidence.com

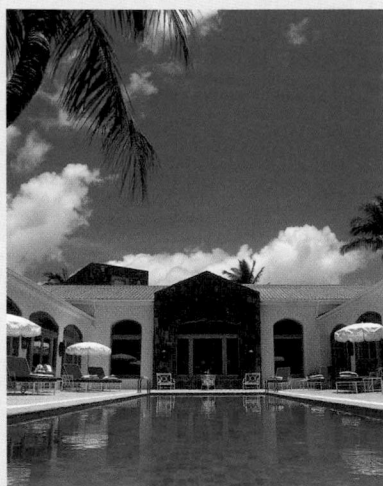
Lap pool at the Givenchy spa, Le Saint Géran

Relax with a drink and be pampered in a top-quality Mauritian spa

Six Senses Spa, Heritage Le Telfair

Tranquil ponds and tropical gardens encircle the seven indoor rooms and two outdoor gazebos at the only six senses spa in Mauritius. With its blend of ancient and modern treatments, it's one for serious spa-goers.
www.heritageletelfair.mu

Source at Legends

Pick from a range of thalassotherapy treatments, Hot Stone therapy for jet lag or an Oriental Beauty Treatment at Legends, built and furnished around the ancient Eastern principles of feng shui.
www.naiade.com

Maradiva Villas Resort & Spa

A small, private retreat for spa buffs and romantics who want to hang out in the private Jacuzzis of the couples' suites. Try one of the signature Indian treatments, such as Samattva, a massage to balance energies and release tensions, an authentic Ayurvedic consultation or the new 'Bootcamp', with yoga.
www.maradiva.com

There is also an increasing number of well-run independent spas around the island, suitable for those on a budget.

TOP FOUR INDEPENDENT SPAS
Gym Hydro Spa, Grand Baie

Offers massages, hammam and sauna.
Tel: 263 4891.
www.grandbaiegym.com. Open: Mon–Sat 8am–8pm. Closed: Sun.

Life Care Spa, Flic en Flac

Eighteen types of massage, including Japanese, Thai and Indian massages and mud baths.
Tel: 453 9999. Email: lifecarespa@yahoo.com

Spa Viva, Quatre Bornes

This spa's Indian head massage is a great antidote to stress.
Tel: 467 8907. Email: spaviva@intnet.mu

Surya, Pereybère

Specialises in Ayurvedic and Thai massage treatments with expert practitioners from India and Thailand.
Tel: 263 1637. www.spasurya.com. Open: daily 9am–7pm.

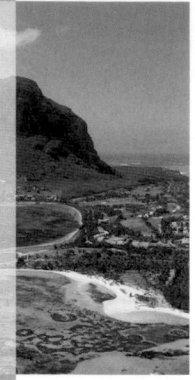

Children

Mauritians love children and you'll find a warm welcome all over the island, from hotel restaurants to the local markets. Increasingly, hotels are offering family-friendly suites and family apartments. The beach is likely to be the main attraction for children here. As the lagoon is largely protected by the coral reef, many of the beaches have long clear shallows that are ideal for toddlers, and as hotels have a plethora of watersports, teens will be equally happy.

The most family-friendly beaches are found at Flic en Flac, Belle Mare, Pereybère and Blue Bay. In addition, there are no venomous snakes or insects on the island and the biggest danger is the sun. Pack plenty of sunblock and a child-friendly mosquito spray.

Kids' clubs

Many hotels on the island organise kids' clubs. Most offer a mix of activities ranging from cooking to nature walks, painting to watersports, as well as supervised trips to the beach and often their own pool and kitchen. Some have teen clubs that have lessons in watersports and a games room.

The following hotels (*see Directory*) all offer kids' clubs and babysitting for an additional fee:

North

Legend's Little Mermaid Club (ages 3–11) and Teens Club (ages 12+)
Maritim's Turtle Club (ages 3–11)
Le Mauricia's Bob Marlin Mini Club (ages 3–12)

Le Méridien's Penguin Children's Club (ages 4–12)
Trou aux Biches' Bob Marlin Mini Club (ages 3–12) and Teens Club (ages 13–16)
Le Victoria's Bob Marlin Mini Club (ages 3–12)

West

La Pirogue's Fun Club (ages 4–12) and Teens Club (ages 12+)

Southwest

Dinarobin's Bob Marlin Mini Club (ages 3–12)
Heritage Awali's Timomo & Friends Mini Club (ages 3–11)
Indian Resort's Akuna Matata Club (ages 3–12)
Le Telfair's Ti Marmite Mini Club (ages 2–11)
Mövenpick Resort & Spa Mini Club (ages 3–12) and Teens Club

East

Beau Rivage's Little Mermaid's Club (ages 3–11) and Teens Club (ages 12+)
Le Touessrok's T-Club (ages 4–11) and Teens Club (ages 12–17)

Southeast
Le Preskil's Kids Club (ages 3–12)
Shandrani's Bob Marlin Mini Club
(ages 3–12)

Great family days out
in five regions
North
L'Aventure du Sucre (*Beau Plan,
Pamplemousses. Tel: 243 7900.
www.aventuredusucre.com*) is an
interesting interactive experience for ten-
year olds and upwards; **Domaine Les
Pailles** (*Les Guibies, Pailles. Tel: 286 4253.
www.domainelespailles.net*) offers
activities for all ages, from pony and
carriage rides to 4WD safari and
trekking, with lunch at an Italian
restaurant overlooking a swimming pool
that children can use. A northern
attraction especially designed for families
is the **Mauritius Aquarium** (*Tel: 261
4561. www.mauritiusaquarium.com*),
with a touch pool, at Pointe aux Piments.
West
A catamaran cruise from Tamarin
to see dolphins (*Croisières Australes.*

*Tel: 263 1669. www.croisieres-
australes.mu*), **Casela Nature and
Leisure Park** (*Tel: 452 0693.
www.caselayemen.mu*) and African
animals zoo for the little ones, and
quad biking in nearby Yemen (*as for
Casela above*) for teenagers – fun for all
the family.
Southwest
Parc Aventure at Chamarel (*Tel: 234
5385/727 0869 (mobile). www.parc-
aventure-chamarel.com*) offers an
army-style obstacle course. Nearby,
at **Frederica Nature Reserve** (*Tel: 623
5615/729 4498 (mobile).
www.domainedebelombre.mu*), there
is a safari by 4WD or quad bike – for
teenagers and young-at-heart adults.
East
Le Waterpark is fun for young
children (*Tel: 415 2626.
www.lewaterpark.intnet.mu*).
Île aux Cerfs has watersports for
teenagers, a pirate boat for youngsters,
and a chance to relax in the shallows
and a gourmet lunch for parents.
Southeast
La Vanille Réserve des Mascareignes
(*Tel: 626 2503. www.lavanille-
reserve.com*) has tortoise rides for
toddlers, crocodiles and monkeys to
keep the older ones amused, and
lunch at The Hungry Crocodile for
all the family.

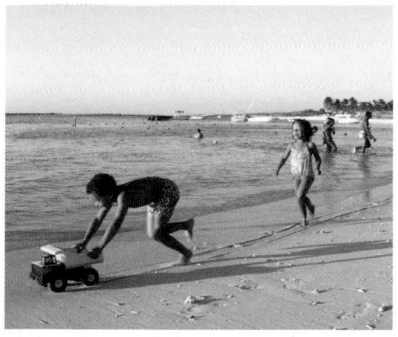
Children will love the island's safe beaches

TRAVELLING

Flights from the UK are generally overnight,
which makes a journey to Mauritius easier to
manage with children.

Essentials

Arriving and departing
Arriving by air
The only international airport in Mauritius is Sir Seewoosagur Ramgoolam International Airport (SSR), or Plaisance Airport, as it's also known (*Code MRU. Tel: 603 6000*), in the southeast of the island. There are only three charter flights to the island: Corsaires flies from France and LTU and Condor from Germany.

Air France *www.airfrance.com*
British Airways *www.ba.com*
Emirates *www.emirates.com*

Air Mauritius (*www.airmauritius.com*) is the main Mauritian carrier, offering direct flights from Paris and London, and over 25 flights a week from several European cities as well as Australia (Perth, Melbourne and Sydney) and South Africa (Johannesburg, Durban and Cape Town). There are no direct flights from the USA, Canada or New Zealand, but going via Asia – Air Mauritius flies direct from Singapore, Malaysia, India and Hong Kong – may offer good deals. Most people coming to Mauritius from the USA or Canada tend to fly via Paris or London.

Flight paths mean that Mauritius can be combined as a twin-centre holiday with a safari in South Africa, Kenya or Botswana, or as a honeymoon following a wedding in the Seychelles.

As an island, there is no approach by rail or road. Very few people arrive by sea, unless on a cruise liner, and a new cruise terminal opened in 2009.

Pick up a map to help direct you to some picturesque routes such as the south coast

Departing by air

Airport departure tax is usually
included in the price of your air
ticket, rather than payable
on departure.

Customs

Visitors aged over 18 can import
duty free:
200 cigarettes or 250g of tobacco
1 litre spirits, 2 litres of wine/beer
250ml of eau de toilette, 100ml
of perfume.

There is no limit on importing
foreign currency, but there is a low
limit on the export of the local
currency, Mauritian rupees.

Electricity

Mauritius uses 220 volts AC for its
supply. Most modern buildings and
hotels, which usually have adaptors
you can borrow, have three-pin plugs,
and budget hotels the two round-
pinned variety.

Internet and email

As Mauritius strives to become a cyber
island, most hotels have high-speed
Internet access and some offer in-room
connection with a laptop. There are
Internet kiosks in many post offices
accessed by a prepaid card bought at
the counter or by credit card. Internet
cafés are usually found in the shopping
arcades of main towns across the
island. The select few listed below are
open from 10am–5pm, and many close
later, although not on Sundays.

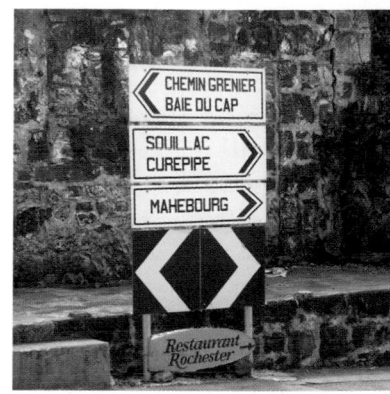

Signs will keep you on the right road

Cyber Café
*Gamefest 10C, Voicy Pougnet Street,
Port Louis. Tel: 208 6369.*
Cyber Café Mosaic
*Royal Road, Quatre Bornes.
Tel: 427 3067.*
Cyber Learning Ltd
*No 2 Centre Commercial La Source,
Centre de Flacq.
Tel: 413 2596.*
Cyber Pirate
*Espace Océan, Royal Road, Grand Baie.
Tel: 263 1757.*
Cyber Power
*F19 1st Floor Manhattan, Curepipe.
Tel: 670 5935.*
Cyber Spot Ltd
303 Royal Road, Rose Hill. Tel: 465 6425.
Cybercaf@Beach Ltd
*Azur Beach Complex Royal Road,
Pereybère.
Tel: 263 4465.*
Cybercafé
*Sans-souci Road, Montagne Blanche.
Tel: 437 4531.*

Maps

The Mauritius Tourism Promotion Authority (MTPA) produces a reasonable *Map of Port Louis & Mauritius*, marked with tourist sites. For something clearer, more detailed and current, pick up the *Tourist Map of Mauritius & Rodrigues* published by Editions Le Printemps Ltée, a bookshop in Vacoas. *Carte Touristique Île Maurice* is produced by the Institut Géographique National (IGN) (*www.ign.fr*), and although more unwieldy, this Ordnance Survey map gives relief and road details.

Money

Currency

The currency used here is the Mauritian rupee. One rupee is made up of 100 cents, with note denominations of Rs25, Rs50, Rs100, Rs200, Rs500, Rs1,000 and Rs2,000 and coins of 5, 20 and 50 cents, and Rs1, Rs5 and Rs10.

Foreign exchange and traveller's cheques

Foreign currency and traveller's cheques can be exchanged at the main banks, bureaux de change and larger hotels. As British tourists are in the majority, pounds sterling are perhaps the best cash choice, but it is also easy to change dollars. Exchange rates are usually better in the country and at banks than at hotels, and no commission is charged for exchanging foreign cash, although there is a charge for traveller's cheques. The main banks on the island are the State Bank of Mauritius (SBM), Mauritius Commercial Bank (MCB), Barclays Bank, Hong Kong and Shanghai Bank (HSBC) and First City Bank. Although rates are similar between them, MCB is rumoured to have the quickest service. ATMs are widespread now in most towns, airports, large supermarkets and shopping malls.

Credit cards

Major credit cards can be used at banks, most hotels, large shops and restaurants, with Visa and Mastercard the most widely accepted. Some establishments add a 2–3 per cent processing fee. Cash advances on major credit cards are available from most of the main banks on presentation of your passport.

Opening hours

Business hours are Monday to Friday 9am–4pm, and Saturday 9am–noon. Banks open Monday to Friday 9.15am–3pm. Post offices open Monday to Friday 8.15am–4pm, and Saturday 8.15am–11.45am. Shops are open Monday to Saturday 9.30am–7.30pm; some open until midday on Sunday. Shops in Rose Hill, Curepipe and Quatre Bournes close on Thursday afternoon. Markets usually close around 4pm. Museums are generally open Monday to Sunday 9.30am–4pm, but are often closed on Tuesday or Wednesday. Check individual attractions' opening hours before setting out.

Passports and visas

Citizens from EU countries, Australia, Canada, New Zealand, South Africa and the USA don't need a visa to enter Mauritius and entry is normally granted for the duration of your stay or up to three months. All visitors need a passport valid for six months and a return or onward ticket.

Pharmacies

Pharmacies are open in the evenings in most towns (look for the green cross) and well stocked with US and European medicines. There are dispensaries and health centres in most villages.

Post

With over 90 post offices scattered throughout Mauritius, there should be no problem finding one nearby. Letters are taken to the post office to post, rather than put in collection boxes. Most hotels will post letters or postcards for you. The postal service in Mauritius is quick and reasonably reliable, with letters or postcards taking about a week to Europe and about ten days to Australia, South Africa and the USA. A poste restante service is available at central post offices.

Public holidays

Mauritius has 15 public holidays a year, although 8 are religious festivals where the dates change each year. These don't affect hotels, but attractions, banks and government buildings will be closed on these days.

The seven fixed holidays are:

1 Jan – New Year's Day
2 Jan – New Year
1 Feb – Abolition of Slavery
12 Mar – National Day
1 May – Labour Day
2 Nov – Arrival of Indentured Labourers
25 Dec – Christmas Day

Smoking

This is forbidden in public places, with smoking and non-smoking sections often found in restaurants. Many hotels operate a no smoking policy in their rooms.

Suggested reading and media
Fiction

A Smile of Fortune and *Twixt Land and Sea* by Joseph Conrad, and *Le Sang des Anglais* by Carl de Souza are all set on the island.
Paul et Virginie by Bernardin de Saint-Pierre is available in English.

Media

There's a weekly English-language newspaper, *News on Sunday*, in Mauritius. TV channels run by Mauritius Broadcasting Company (MBC) have local news bulletins in English at 7am and 9pm, but Mauritius College of the Air (MCA) television tends to have more English programmes. Most hotels and resorts have satellite TV, including the news on Sky, CNN and BBC World.

Non-fiction

The Dive Sites of Mauritius by Alan
Mountain (Struik, 1996).
Comprehensive.
Dodo – the Bird behind the Legend by
Alan Grihault (IPC Ltd, Mauritius,
2005). The definitive guide to
Mauritius' most famous icon.
Golden Bats and pink pigeons by Gerald
Durrell (Fountain, 1979). Informative
and entertaining.
Last Chance to See by Douglas Adams
and Mark Carwardine (Heinemann,
London, 1990). Includes a good section
on birds of the Mascarenes.

Tax

Fifteen per cent value-added tax (VAT)
is payable on goods and services,
including hotel and restaurant bills,
although hotels tend to include this in
the price of rooms. In restaurants, a
footnote will stipulate whether VAT is
included or not. As Mauritius is a duty-
free shopping centre, VAT paid on

Temples of all shapes and sizes are found
across the island in unusual places

duty-free goods can be claimed back at
the airport.

Telephones

Over 600 public payphones using coins
or prepay phonecards are installed
throughout Mauritius, at bus stations,
shopping centres or even in small
corner shops, although they may not
always work. *Télécartes* (phonecards)
are indicated by stickers and samples of
cards displayed in shop windows. These
will include bookshops, supermarkets
and news vendors or even fast-food
snack bars in busy towns. **Mauritius
Telecom** (*www.mauritiustelecom.com*)
offers a good, reliable service, and
payphones are found in their customer
service centres in towns around the
island. Of companies that offer prepaid
phonecards giving a much better rate
for international calls, the most popular
is Mauritius Telecoms Sezam. Others
are Yellow or Allo; Cell Plus and Emtel
cards are more expensive for
international calls.

All large hotels and resorts will have
international direct dialling, usually
above the usual rate and sometimes
extremely expensive. The country code
for Mauritius from overseas is *230*.
To make an international call from
Mauritius, simply dial *00* followed by
the country code; for example:
Australia *00 61*
New Zealand *00 64*
South Africa *00 27*
UK *00 44*
USA and Canada *00 1*

Mauritius has good mobile phone coverage. Mobile networks use the European GSM system, which means that you can activate a 'roaming' account if your phone is compatible. If you decide to rent a local mobile, local calls cost the same as from a landline. Contact your mobile provider for more details.

Time

Mauritius is GMT + 4 hours. In the British winter, when it's noon in Mauritius it's 8am in London, 7pm in Sydney, 3am in New York and Toronto, and 10am in Johannesburg.

Tipping

There are no rigid guidelines as to how much to tip; it's discretionary. Tipping is not expected (except in hotels and tourist establishments), but appreciated.

Toilets

Mauritius doesn't have an over-generous provision of public toilets. You will find good ones at public beaches, attractions and in the newer shopping arcades. Otherwise, it's a friendly place, so try asking at cafés, hotels and restaurants.

Tourist information

The Mauritius Tourism Promotion Authority (MTPA) has its head office and an information office on the 11th Floor of the Air Mauritius Building (*John Kennedy Street, Port Louis, Mauritius. Tel: 210 1545. www.tourism-mauritius.mu*). There's a tourist information office on the ground floor. There is a surprising scarcity of tourist information offices around the island, but they can be found at Trou d'Eau Douce and at the airport. Free tourist booklets and leaflets produced by the MTPA include: *Mauritius & Rodrigues information guide*; *Rodrigues – your guide*; *What's on in Mauritius* (annually); *Diving in Mauritius*; *Map of Port Louis & Mauritius*; and *Mauritius Green Map*.

Travellers with disabilities

Many hotels claim to have facilities for people with disabilities, but some cater better than others. It's always best to check exactly what is offered before booking. Although main towns are accessible, some of the beach resorts have limited paving. Public transport doesn't cater well for travellers with disabilities, who may be forced to rely on tourist minibuses and taxis. Domaine Les Pailles (*see p41*) is one attraction with full wheelchair access; a newly built conference centre and the Caudan Waterfront (*see p27*) have ramps and lifts, making some concessions to those with disabilities.

Useful numbers

Airline departures/arrivals: *Tel: 603 3030 (Air Mauritius); 603 6000 (other airlines)*
Tourist information: *Tel: 210 1545*
Tourist police: *Tel: 210 3894*
Directory enquiries: *Tel: 150*
Operator: *Tel: 150*
International operator: *Tel: 10090*

Language

Although English is the official language, Mauritian Creole (MC or Morisyen) dominates everyday life, and most people speak French too. In the tourist industry and in business circles, everyone speaks fluent English as well as other European languages such as Italian, German and Spanish. English is also used on traffic signs.

Most Creole words evolved from the pidgin French of the old plantation slaves, words like *liver* (winter) from the French *l'hiver*, and *dilo* (water) from the French *de l'eau*. Other languages have found their way into the mix – over 150 words are derived from English, more than 50 from Indian languages, and several from Malagasy and Chinese. Mauritian people will be both surprised and pleased if you learn any Creole phrases, and it will help with bargaining in the market. Creole dictionaries such as *Parlez Créole/Speak Creole* by Rose Hill (Mauritius: Éditions de L'Océan Indien) are on sale in Mauritius. The following phrases (the Creole is spelt phonetically) will give you a headstart:

PHRASES

English	Creole	French
Good morning	Bonzour	Bonjour
Goodbye	Bye/salam/ore revwar	Au revoir
How are you?	Kee Manyeer?	Comment ça va?
Are you okay?	Sava?	Est-ce que ça va?
I'm okay, thank you	Bien mersi	Ça va bien, merci
Okay	Corek	D'accord
Please	Siupleh	S'il vous plaît
Thank you	Mersi	Merci
My name is	Mo appel	Je m'appelle
What is your name?	Coma oua peleh?	Comment vous appellez-vous?

English	Creole	French
I want…	Mo ouleh…	Je veux…
Where is…	Cotte…	Où est…
I like…	Mo conton…	J'aime…
It's good	Le bon sa	C'est bon
How much is it?	Comyeh?	Combien?
It's expensive	Sai Sa	C'est cher
Market	Bazar	Le marché
Supermarket	Sipairmarseh	Le supermarché
Chemist	La farmasi	La pharmacie
Post office	Le pos	Le bureau de poste
Stamp	Teim	Un timbre
Restaurant	Le restoran	Le restaurant
I'm hungry	Mofen	J'ai faim
I'm thirsty	Mo swaf	J'ai soif
Beer	La bier	La bière
Wine	Dee vin	Du vin
Tea with milk	Diteh avec dileh	Thé au lait
Waiters	Servair	Garçons
Hotel	Lotel	L'hôtel
Clean	Netwayeh	Nettoyer
Towel	Serviet	Serviette
I'm not well	Mo pas bien	Je ne me sens pas bien
I need a doctor	Mo bisin en doktere	J'ai besoin d'un médecin

SLANG

English	Creole
Very good	Vari bon sa
Hang out	Chakeh
Cool	Kul

Emergencies

Emergency telephone numbers

Fire: *999*
Ambulance: *114*
Police: *558 13/20*
Weather information during
cyclones: *96*

Health

Mauritius doesn't have malaria, and
no vaccinations are required to visit.
The most serious problem here is the
danger of contracting Chikungunya, a
viral disease transmitted by mosquitoes.
Although the government are spraying
to reduce breeding, visitors need to be
liberal with the insect repellent to
prevent biting, even in the day, and
particularly in the warmer months
(October–May). The only other
problem may be an encounter with
a pack of stray dogs, but rabies is
not a risk here.

It is always recommended that you
take out comprehensive travel and
health insurance, with particular
regard to covering any activities you
wish to undertake, and emergency
repatriation cover if you consider
yourself at risk of serious illness.
However, there is a good general
standard of health care in the private
clinics found across the island, and
these provide day-to-day medical
services for a reasonable fee. There are
also a couple of good public hospitals
should you need them.

Clinics
City Clinic, *Sir Edgar Laurent Street,
Port Louis. Tel: 241 2951.*
Clinic Darné, *George Guibert Street,
Floréal. Tel: 601 2300.*
www.cliniquedarne.com
Clinic du Nord, *Coast Road, Baie du
Tombeau. Tel: 247 2532.*

Hospitals
**Sir Seewoosagur Ramgoolam
National Hospital**, *Pamplemousses.
Tel: 243 3661.*
Dr Jettoo Hospital, *Volcy Pougnet
Street, Port Louis. Tel: 212 3201.*

There are no venomous reptiles or
dangerous animals on the island.
However, take precautions against
the following sea creatures during
your stay:
Sea urchins: Avoid walking on these
as their spines are very hard to remove
once embedded in your foot and can
be infectious.
Stonefish: Although few are found
on the island and hotels monitor their
own beaches, this fish lies motionless
and camouflaged on the sandy bottom
of the sea. If you step on one, you
should be treated urgently, as the
venom can be fatal.
Lionfish: This distinctive-looking
red and white, slow-moving fish
has venomous fins that it fans out
and should not be touched.

Crime and scams

Although Mauritius has a low crime rate, there is petty crime in the capital's crowded market and main tourist centre, Grand Baie. Break-ins to self-catering accommodation are not unknown, and lone women travellers should exercise caution and avoid walking alone at night. An unobtrusive tourist police operates in tourist zones to ensure the safety of visitors.

Follow the Mauritius Tourism Promotion Authority (MTPA) guidelines below to help ensure your safety and security on holiday:

- Keep an eye on all personal belongings at all times.
- Be careful when withdrawing money from an ATM.
- Avoid wearing expensive jewellery.
- Don't leave anything inside your car.
- For trips or purchases, use only recognised operators or suppliers.
- Keep your passports, plane tickets, jewellery and large sums of money in safes.
- During individual sea journeys, notify the person responsible for the boat if you encounter problems.
- For sea excursions, don't rent boats with inadequate security standards.

HOLIDAY HAIR TRANSPLANT?

The **Hairgrafting Centre** in Mauritius is one of the three most advanced clinics for this technique in the world and costs between 40–60 per cent less than in Europe.
Centre médical de greffe de cheveux, Pointe aux Canonniers. Tel: 265 5050. www.calvitie.net

---

- Don't go swimming in areas where it is forbidden, which are clearly marked around the island.

Note that drug trafficking in Mauritius carries a heavy penalty. For the latest information on travel health and safety in Mauritius, check the Foreign & Commonwealth travel advice at *www.fco.gov.uk*

Embassies and consulates

All embassies and consulates are situated in the capital, Port Louis.

Australian High Commission
2nd Floor, Rogers House, 5 President John Kennedy Street. Tel: 202 0160. www.mauritius.embassy.gov.au

British High Commission
7th Floor, Les Cascades Building, Edith Cavell Street. Tel: 202 9400. http://ukinmauritius.fco.gov.uk

Canadian Consulate
18 Jules Koenig Street. Tel: 212 5500.

New Zealand Consulate
Anchor Building, Les Pailles, Bell Village. Tel: 286 4920.

South African High Commission
4th Floor, BAI Building, 25 Pope Hennessy Street. Tel: 212 6925.

US Embassy
4th Floor, Rogers House, 5 President John Kennedy Street. Tel: 202 4400.

Directory

Accommodation price guide

Prices of accommodation are based on a double room per night for two people sharing, with breakfast.

£	up to Rs3,000
££	Rs3,000–Rs8,000
£££	Rs8,000–Rs18,000
££££	over Rs18,000

Eating out price guide

Prices are based on an average three-course meal for one, without drinks.

£	up to Rs700
££	Rs700–Rs1,000
£££	over Rs1,000

NORTH

Anse La Raie

ACCOMMODATION

Le Paradise Cove Hotel & Spa £££

Small, family-run hotel in an Indian-romantic style. Dinner is in thatched huts on stilts over the lagoon. No young children allowed.
Anse La Raie.
Tel: 204 4000. www. paradisecovehotel.com

Grand Baie

ACCOMMODATION

Hôtel 20° Sud/Hotel 20° South ££

Boutique hotel in a quiet coconut grove on the waterfront. Family-run and good value for money. No children under 12.
Coastal Road, Pointe Malartic. Tel: 263 5000.
www.20degressud.com

Le Mauricia ££

This 4-star hotel has excellent dining, land- and watersports, a dive centre, a spa and its own nightclub. Each room is sea-facing with a balcony. The Mauricia Village apartments are for families. All-inclusive options available.
Royal Road. Tel: 209 1100.
www.lemauricia-hotel.com

Trou aux Biches Resort & Spa ££££

This village-style resort opened after a two-year rebuild on the site of the old Coco Beach Hotel in 2010, with suites and villas with private plunge pools and one of the best beaches on the island. Six restaurants, kids' clubs, Clarins spa and mostly complimentary land- and watersports.

Triolet, Nr Grand Baie.
Tel: 204 6800. www. beachcomber-hotels.com

EATING OUT

Don Camillo £

A well-priced, informal Italian restaurant.
Coastal Road.
Tel: 263 8540.

La Terrasse ££

Chinese, Creole and European cuisine is served in this cosy and affordable family-run restaurant with sea views and outdoor dining option.
Royal Road. Tel: 263 6391. Open: for lunch and dinner. Closed: Tue.

Le Capitaine £££

Great seafood in a romantic setting.
Coastal Road. Tel: 263 7526. Open: daily, lunch and dinner. Book ahead.

ENTERTAINMENT
The Banana Café
A favourite frequented by tourists and locals. Live music at weekends and DJ 10pm–2am.
Royal Road. Tel: 263 0326.
Zanzibar Nightclub
A place to head for a good time after the bars and restaurants close.
Royal Road. Tel: 256 5659.

SPORT AND LEISURE
Croisières Australes
Catamaran cruises in Tamarin Bay, to Île aux Cerfs and the Northern Islands.
Coastal Road.
Tel: 263 1669. www. croisieres-australes.mu

Grand Gaube
ACCOMMODATION
Legends £££
The only hotel on the island designed to feng shui principles, with lots of watersports on offer, rooms in bold colours and a great view to the Northern Islands.
Pointe Réjane, Tel: 204 9191. www.naiade.com

SPORT AND LEISURE
Yemaya Adventures
Led by previous cycling and kayaking champion Patrick Haberland, Yemaya Adventures arranges mountain biking, sea-kayaking and hiking.
Grand Gaube.
Tel: 752 0046. www. yemayaadventures.com

Pointe aux Canonniers
ACCOMMODATION
Le Canonnier Hotel £££
A 4-star contemporary hotel offering good-value, all-inclusive packages aimed at families. It also has 21 apartments.
Royal Road. Tel: 209 7000. www.lecanonnier-hotel.com
Club Med £££
With Creole architecture, the hotel offers a host of activities from glass bottom boat trips to waterskiing or sailing lessons. A great choice for active families.
Pointe aux Canonniers. Tel: 209 1000. www.clubmed.com

Pointe aux Piments
ACCOMMODATION
Le Méridien £££
A big hotel on a lovely long stretch of beach. All 198 large rooms and suites overlook the bay. As well as all the usual facilities, it has its own diving centre, shopping arcade and spa. All-inclusive packages available.
Village Hall Lane.
Tel: 204 3333.
www.lemeridien.com
Le Victoria £££
Le Victoria is a family-friendly hotel offering all-inclusive packages. It has three restaurants, a large swimming pool close to the sea and plenty of watersports.
Pointe aux Piments.
Tel: 204 2000.
www.levictoria-hotel.com

SPORT AND LEISURE
Exotic Cruise Ltd
Parasailing over the northern coast, from Grand Baie.
Royal Road. Tel: 261 1724.

Port Louis and surrounds
EATING OUT
Chez Tante Athalie £
This restaurant frequented by locals serves a *prix fixe* Creole lunch which changes daily, on the terrace overlooking a garden full of vintage cars.
Next to Pamplemousses

Gdns. *Tel: 243 9266. Email: cheztanteathalie@ intnet.mu. Open: Mon–Sat noon–2.30pm.*

Le Café du Vieux Conseil ££

This is a popular spot for a Creole lunch in an open-air courtyard. *Vieux Conseil Street. Tel: 211 0393. Open: for lunch only 11am–3pm. Closed: Sun.*

Le Fangourin ££

The restaurant at L'Aventure du Sucre specialises in Seychelles fish dishes but also has good regional dishes. *Beau Plan, Pamplemousses. Tel: 243 7900. www.aventuredusucre.com. Open: daily 9am–5pm.*

Namasté ££

An authentic Indian restaurant, with live music at weekends. *Caudan Waterfront. Tel: 211 6710. Open: daily 11am–3.30pm & 6.30– 10.30pm. Book ahead.*

Domaine Les Pailles ££–£££

Ten minutes' drive south of Port Louis, Domaine Les Pailles offers four restaurants. **La Dolce Vita** Italian restaurant is the least expensive for lunch

and has music at weekends (*Open: Wed, Fri & Sat for dinner*). The **Indra** Indian restaurant with live *tabla* music, is one of the island's best and is more expensive (*Closed: Sun*). Other choices are **Fu Xiao** Chinese restaurant (*Closed: Sat lunch*), and **Clos Saint Louis**, which serves Mauritian lunches in a replica of a colonial home (*Closed: Sat*). *Pailles. Tel: 286 4225. www.domainelespailles.net*

Le Pescatore Restaurant £££

One of the best gourmet fish restaurants. Dine on the veranda overlooking the ocean. *Coastal Road, Trou aux Biches. Tel: 265 6337.*

ENTERTAINMENT

Le Grand Casino du Domaine

This is the nicest casino in Mauritius. *Domaine Les Pailles. Tel: 286 0407. www. casinosofmauritius.com. Open: daiy 8pm–4am.*

The Palladium Nightclub

Dance spot in a Roman-style villa.

Trianon, near Port Louis. Tel: 454 6168.

Star Cinema

Three-screen cinema showing Western films. *Caudan Waterfront. Tel: 211 5361.*

SPORT AND LEISURE

Centre Equestre de la Louisa

Some 60 horses and ponies are available for one-hour lessons to day-long trail rides through the sugar-cane fields; beach rides can also be arranged. Caters for children 3 and upwards. *Bellevue, Pamplemousses. Tel: 739 1410. Trail ride Mon–Sat 9.30am.*

Les Écuries du Domaine Les Pailles

Pony riding for children 3–12 years old. *Pailles. Tel: 286 4253. www.domainelespailles. net. Open: Mon–Sat from 7.30am–5pm.*

Terre Rouge

ACCOMMODATION

Maritim Hotel Mauritius £££

The stunning bar is a main feature of this vibrant hotel set in tropical gardens in Turtle

Bay. The rooms are decked out in tropical colours. Good snorkelling, a spa, a nine-hole golf course and equestrian centre.
Balaclava. Tel: 204 1000. www.maritim.com

WEST
Curepipe
SPORT AND LEISURE
Vertical World
Mountain climbing, trekking and canyoning.
Curepipe. Tel: 254 6607. www.verticalworldltd.com

Flic en Flac
ACCOMMODATION
La Pirogue £££
One of the oldest hotels in Mauritius, La Pirogue has kept its uniqueness. One of the best on the island for families.
Wolmar. Tel: 403 3900. www.lapirogue.com

The Sands Resort & Spa £££
With 91 deluxe seafront rooms and one suite, this is a lovely, serene 3-star hotel tucked away at the quieter end of Flic en Flac with spa and PADI dive centre.
Wolmar. Tel: 403 1200. www.thesandsresort.mu

Sugar Beach Resort £££
Grand colonial building on the longest white-sand beach on the island. It has colonial-style dark-wood rooms, a spa and a beachside seafood restaurant. All-inclusive packages are available.
Wolmar. Tel: 403 3300. www.sugarbeachresort.com

Maradiva Villas Resort & Spa ££££
With 65 luxury villas and guaranteed 5-star pampering in exquisite surroundings, think 24-hour butler service, plunge pool and giant bed with great bathroom.
Wolmar. Tel: 403 1500. www.maradiva.com

EATING OUT
Domaine Anna Restaurant ££
In the sugar-cane fields, Domaine Anna is most spectacular at dinner. Torches are lit along the drive, and groups can opt for one of the gazebos on the lakes. Live music and dancing at weekends.
Médine. Tel: 453 9650. www.domaineanna.net. Open: Tue–Sun 11.30am–2.30pm & 6.30–10.30pm. Closed: Mon.

Moka
ACCOMMODATION
Eureka ££
The three peaceful guest rooms facing the mountain are set in lovely gardens away from the main house.
La Maison Creole, Eureka. Tel: 433 8477. www.maisoneureka.com

Rivière Noire
SPORT AND LEISURE
Otélair Ltée
Mountain climbing, hiking, canyoning and trekking.
Tel: 696 6750. www.otelair.com

Vacoas
SPORT AND LEISURE
Gymkhana Club Golf Course
The oldest 18-hole golf course on the island, built in 1902 for the Royal Navy.
Suffolk Road. Tel: 696 2050. www.mgc.intnet.mu

SOUTHWEST
Bel Ombre
ACCOMMODATION
Heritage Awali Golf and Spa Resort £££
A good 4-star in a new clutch of hotels, this

resort has an African-inspired spa and warm, rich décor as well as an 18-hole golf course, kids' club, restaurants, tennis courts and three pools. *Bel Ombre. Tel: 266 9777. www.heritageawali.mu*

Mövenpick Resort & Spa £££
Awarded the accolade of 'leading family resort in the Indian Ocean' in 2008, the Mövenpick is a good-value, spacious 4-star resort with a shopping mall, four swimming pools, a great spa and large bedrooms with whirlpools and outdoor showers. *Bel Ombre. Tel: 623 5000. www.moevenpick-hotels.com*

Tamassa £££
This funky, vibrant 4-star resort, set on a coconut-fringed white-sand beach, is one of the newest to have opened in the southwest. Includes a kids' and teens' club, dive centre, luxury spa and four swimming pools. *Bel Ombre. Tel: 603 7300. www.naiade.com*

Heritage Le Telfair ££££
A 'small luxury hotel of the world', this hotel reflects the colonial grandeur of a Mauritius past. The spa is one of the best on the island, as is the golf course, and it has a kids' club, watersports, restaurants and a big pool. Activities range from quad biking to tai-chi. *Bel Ombre. Tel: 601 5500. www.heritageletelfair.mu. com*

So Mauritius ££££
Sofitel's new 5-star hotel is the height of 'eco-chic'. All in white with splashes of lime, its 92 suites and villas have private gardens, plunge pools and butlers. A stunning cathedral-like area houses a Michelin-starred restaurant and bar, and there's a large pool. *Bel Ombre. Tel: 483 5043. www.sofitel.com*

EATING OUT
Le Château de Bel Ombre ££–£££
This elegant restaurant is in a beautifully restored building dating back to the early 1800s. Provides a good-value *prix fixe* Mauritian lunch and an à la carte dinner. It's being renovated, so check that it's open before visiting. *Tel: 623 5622. www. domainedebelombre.mu*

SPORT AND LEISURE
Chazal
Tyrolienne and zipline adventure. *Chamonix, east of Bel Ombre. Tel: 622 7234 or 422 3117/3120 (mobiles).*

Golf du Château, Bel Ombre
Built between the mountains and the sea, this award-winning 18-hole golf course was designed by Peter Matkovitch. There are nine beginners' holes. *Le Telfair. Tel: 601 5500. www.heritageletelfair.mu. Heritage: Tel: 601 1500. www.heritageawali.mu. Open: daily 7am–4pm.*

Chamarel
ACCOMMODATION
Les Écuries de la Vieille Cheminée ££
Self-catering accommodation in a 121ha (300-acre) estate. Guests stay in three rustic Creole-style chalets with horse riding, cycling and guided walks. *Chamarel. Tel: 483 5249 or 725 5546 (mobile). www. lavieillecheminee.com*

EATING OUT
Le Chamarel
Restaurant ££
There are stunning
views over Le Morne and
Île aux Bénitiers.
Although it serves rather
average Mauritian
specialities, it's worth it
for the view.
La Crete. Tel: 483 6421.
Open: daily for lunch
(noon–3pm). Book ahead.

Le Morne Peninsula
ACCOMMODATION
Indian Resort £££
The Indian resort offers
something for both action
and relaxation in 11ha (27
acres) of tropical gardens.
The beach has kite-surfing
at one end and a quiet
area at the other. The
resort offers good value
in a beautiful setting, but
has been undergoing
renovation. Check before
booking.
Le Morne Peninsula.
Tel: 401 4200.
www.apavou-hotels.com
Dinarobin Hotel Golf
& Spa ££££
This recently renovated
172-suite hotel has
arguably the most
dramatic and romantic
spot on the island. It has

a 7km (4-mile) white-
sand beach, a wonderful
Clarins spa and Creole
cookery courses.
Le Morne Peninsula.
Tel: 401 4900.
www.dinarobin-hotel.com

EATING OUT
Le Varangue sur
Morne ££
An open-sided lunch
spot with wooden floor
and tables as well as a
stupendous view (ask for
the corner balcony
table). It has a *prix fixe*
buffet lunch and an
imaginative à la carte
menu, and optional
helicopter arrival.
Coeur Bois, near
Le Morne. Tel: 483 6610.
www.acoeurbois.com
Open: daily for lunch.
Dinner by reservation.

SPORT AND LEISURE
Club Mistral, Indian
Resort
Kite-surfing for beginners
and advanced.
Le Morne. Tel: 450 4112.
www.club-mistral.com
Yanature Adventures
Mountain climbing,
trekking and trail
running with naturalist
Yan de Maroussem.

Tel: 785 6177. www.
trekkingilemaurice.com

Port Souillac
EATING OUT
Le Batelage £
In an old sugar mill on
the mouth of a river, with
seafood specialities.
Village des Touristes.
Tel: 625 6083. Email:
lebatelage@intnet.mu.
Open: daily 11am–6pm.
Dinner reservations
required.

Rivière des Anguilles
ACCOMMODATION
Le Saint Aubin ££
This is a chance to stay
in a four-poster bed in
your own wooden-
shuttered colonial
residence among
birdsong in tropical
gardens. Just one double
and two family rooms
have access to a dining
area, large veranda and
small swimming pool.
Half-board mandatory.
Rivière des Anguilles.
Tel: 626 1730.
www.saintaubin.mu

EATING OUT
Le Saint Aubin ££
A quality Creole set table
d'hôte lunch in elegant

colonial surrounds with good service.
See above. Tel: 626 1513.

EAST
Belle Mare
ACCOMMODATION
La Palmeraie ££
La Palmeraie is in a good spot right on Belle Mare beach (a top kite-surfing location), near the elegant Residence Hotel. With a Moorish feel, this intimate 4-star hotel is both serene and different.
Coastal Road.
Tel: 401 8500.
www.hotel-palmeraie.com
Beau Rivage £££
Beautifully situated on the beach, what's really unique about this hotel are its themed suites – Indian, African, Chinese – each one exquisitely decorated.
Belle Mare. Tel: 402 2000.
www.naiade.com
Long Beach £££
This 5-star hotel opened in spring 2011. Its 255 ocean-view rooms arranged in crescents bring Ibiza-style living to one of the east coast's most stunning beaches. Facilities range from a spa to a kids' club.

Coastal Road.
Tel: 419 1919. www. longbeachmauritius.com

EATING OUT
Mon Repos ££
Recommended by locals and expats, this restaurant serves typical Mauritian food such as Biryiani and Rougaille. Dine inside or outside.
Trianon, Quatre Bornes. Tel: 465 8403.
Symon's Restaurant ££
Offering a selection of Chinese, Indian Creole or seafood.
Coastal Road.
Tel: 415 1135. Open: daily 11am–midnight.

SPORT AND LEISURE
Ernie Els Golf Course
This 18-hole championship golf course is one of the latest to hit the island.
Anahita, Grand Rivière Sud-Est. Tel: 402 2200.
www.anahita.mu

Post de Flacq
ENTERTAINMENT
Laguna Bar, Le Prince Maurice
Blow the budget on the signature cocktail of

perhaps the grandest hotel on the island.
Poste de Flacq.
Tel: 402 3636.
www.princemaurice.com

Trou d'Eau Douce
ACCOMMODATION
Le Touessrok ££££
Understated luxury on a spectacular site spread over three idyllic islands. A short boat ride away is Île aux Cerfs Golf Course and Îlot Mangenie, a Robinson Crusoe-type getaway. Dine on cuisines from eight countries at the excellent Three-Nine-Eight restaurant and be pampered at the Givenchy Spa.
Trou d'Eau Douce.
Tel: 402 7400.
www.letouessrokresort.com

EATING OUT
Paul et Virginie ££
An elegant restaurant specialising in grills, seafood, pizzas and a variety of Mauritian dishes.
Trou d'Eau Douce.
Book through Le Touessrok Hotel.
Tel: 402 7400.
www.letouessrokresort.com.
Open: daily noon–3pm.

SPORT AND LEISURE
Le Touessrok Golf Course

Fringed by white sands and with a backdrop of green mountains, this has been voted one of the world's most stunning golf settings.
Île aux Cerfs. Tel: 402 7720/7400. www. letouessrokresort.com. Open: daily 6.40am–6pm.

SOUTHEAST
Anse Jonchée
ACCOMMODATION
Ti Vilaz, The Kestrel Valley ££

Seven African-style thatched huts perch in this peaceful nature park atop the hill, with a stunning view to the sea. Don't forget the insect repellent!
Anse Jonchée. Tel: 634 5097. www.kestrelvalley.com

EATING OUT
Le Panoramour, The Kestrel Valley ££

Perched 300m (984ft) up a hill, with a fantastic view of the southeast coast and an adventurous game menu.
Anse Jonchée. Tel: 634 5097. www.kestrelvalley.com. Open: daily 10am–3.30pm.

Blue Bay
ACCOMMODATION
Blue Lagoon Beach Hotel ££

With friendly staff and all-inclusive packages, this 72-room hotel is a good-value option near the Blue Bay Marine Park and Mahébourg. It is only ten minutes from the airport, so it suffers a bit from aeroplane noise.
Blue Bay. Tel: 631 9046. www. bluelagoonbeachhotel.com

Shandrani £££

A luxury all-inclusive hotel on a double stretch of beach and within a 20ha (50-acre) garden. With a large selection of sports and activities, it is great for the active and adventurous. The only downside is that it is close to airport noise.
Blue Bay. Tel: 603 4343. www.shandrani-resort.com

SPORT AND LEISURE
Beachcomber Sport & Nature

Land- and watersports can be arranged through this hotel and the Shandrani.
Shandrani Hotel. Tel: 603 4343. www.beachcomber-hotels.com

The Shandrani Hotel

This kite-surfing school is perfect for beginners.
Blue Bay. Tel: 603 4343. www.shandrani-resort.com

Vieux Grand Port
EATING OUT
Le Barachois ££

A rustic stone restaurant with stick fences and thatch, coral underfoot and shells on the wall, Le Barachois specialises in giant prawns, lobster and crab farmed here.
Anse Bambous, Vieux Grand Port. Tel: 634 5643. Email: le.barachois@yahoo.com. Open: daily 9am–5pm for lunch. Booking necessary only for early dinner.

La Belle Kréole ££

In this atmospheric authentic Creole restaurant in a stunning spot by the river, local women prepare the food over a wood-burning fire. You are offered a boat trip while waiting for your beautifully presented meal.
Coastal Road, Pointe d'Esny. Tel: 631 5017. Open: daily 10am–3pm & 6–11pm.

Index

Acknowledgements

Thomas Cook Publishing wishes to thank NICKI GRIHAULT, to whom the copyright belongs, for the photographs in this book, except for the following images:

ACCOR IMAGE BANK 117
BEACHCOMBER HOTELS 125
BLUE SAFARI SUBMARINE 39
MTPA 1, 4, 15, 17, 23, 38, 111, 137, 140
ONE&ONLY RESORTS 16, 112, 113 (P Tosselli), 34 (J B Adoue), 115 (Chris Tubbs), 124 (R Starr), 136 (J Nicholson)
www.bigfoto.com 86
YEMAYA ADVENTURES 103

For CAMBRIDGE PUBLISHING MANAGEMENT LIMITED:
Project editor: Rosalind Munro
Typesetter: Paul Queripel
Proofreaders: Jan McCann & Caroline Hunt

SEND YOUR THOUGHTS TO
BOOKS@THOMASCOOK.COM

We're committed to providing the very best up-to-date information in our travel guides and constantly strive to make them as useful as they can be. You can help us to improve future editions by letting us have your feedback. If you've made a wonderful discovery on your travels that we don't already feature, if you'd like to inform us about recent changes to anything that we do include, or if you simply want to let us know your thoughts about this guidebook and how we can make it even better – we'd love to hear from you.

Send us ideas, discoveries and recommendations today and then look out for your valuable input in the next edition of this title.

Emails to the above address, or letters to the traveller guides Series Editor, Thomas Cook Publishing, PO Box 227, Coningsby Road, Peterborough PE3 8SB, UK.

Please don't forget to let us know which title your feedback refers to!

R.C.L.

JAN. 2012

G